# HEALING ZEN

# HEALING ZEN

*Awakening to a Life*
*of Wholeness and Compassion*
*While Caring for Yourself*
*and Others*

## ELLEN BIRX
*Ph.D., R.N.*

VIKING COMPASS

VIKING COMPASS
Published by the Penguin Group
Penguin Putnam Inc., 375 Hudson Street, New York, New York 10014, U. S. A.
Penguin Books Ltd, 80 Strand, London WC2R 0RL, England
Penguin Books Australia Ltd, Ringwood, Victoria, Australia
Penguin Books Canada Ltd, 10 Alcorn Avenue,
Toronto, Ontario, Canada M4V 3B2
Penguin Books (N.Z.) Ltd, 182–190 Wairau Road, Auckland 10, New Zealand

Penguin Books Ltd, Registered Offices:
Harmondsworth, Middlesex, England

First published in 2002 by Viking Compass,
a member of Penguin Putnam Inc.

1   3   5   7   9   10   8   6   4   2

Line drawings by Laura Hartman Maestro

Library of Congress Cataloging-in-Publication Data
Birx, Ellen.
Healing Zen / Ellen Birx.
p.   cm.
ISBN 0-670-03053-8
1. Spiritual life—Zen Buddhism   2. Healing—Religious aspects—Zen Buddhism.
I. Title.
BQ9288 .B57 2002
294.3'731—dc21                    2001035207

This book is printed on acid-free paper. ∞

Printed in the United States of America
Set in Fournier
Designed by Francesca Belanger

*To my teacher*
*Roshi Robert Jinsen Kennedy*

# Acknowledgments

Special thanks go to my husband Charles whom I have loved for thirty-five years. His strong Zen meditation practice over the years inspired me to keep going. He enthusiastically read the manuscript and offered many helpful suggestions.

I thank all my family and friends especially my bright, beautiful daughter Clare and my sweet, lively granddaughter Brenna who provided many enjoyable and refreshing breaks from writing. I am grateful for my mother Kathleen who always encouraged all of her five children to pursue their interests whatever they may be.

My heartfelt thanks go to my Zen teacher Roshi Robert Jinsen Kennedy, his teacher Roshi Bernard Tetsugen Glassman, and to all the Zen teachers who came before them for keeping Zen alive and available in the world. I also thank the members of New River Zen Community and all the friends I have been practicing Zen with for many years, especially Rosemary O'Connell, Jim and Carol Grealish, Fran and Greg Rooker, Marty White, Marsha Dubose, Pat Shoemaker, Jan Hencke, Ben Pumphrey, Monica Appleby, Germille Colmano, and Jeanne Roper.

I am very grateful to my energetic agent Carol Susan

Roth for making this book a reality. I would like to express my great appreciation for my outstanding editor Janet Goldstein and her assistant Ann Mah, who were both highly skilled and warmly supportive.

And finally I thank my nursing colleagues, students, and patients who taught me what I know about healing.

# Contents

## II. Vital Signs: Changes That Come
### Through Healing  ❋  87

III. Compassionate Action: Reaching Out
   with Healing Hands   ❋   169

# Preface

*Healing Zen* is for caregivers, patients, and anyone who feels the need for healing. It is offered to give insight and encouragement regarding the human experience of illness, healing, and wholeness in everyday life. As a nurse, I work on a daily basis helping people during difficult times in their lives. I experience firsthand the physical demands of caregiving: the lifting, cleaning, and standing at the bedside of people in their hour of greatest need. For me Zen practice is a way to restore my energy and build the endurance needed in many caregiving situations. It also provides me with the depth of psychological and spiritual insight I need to sustain me as I care for people facing life's hardest issues like fear, pain, dependence, loss, and death. In my own life and in the lives of other professional and family caregivers who I have shared Zen practice with, Zen is a simple yet profound way to nourish and care for the caregiver. Zen practice awakens me to the richness and fullness of life and helps me be more alive, joyful, and intimate.

Zen is not dogma, doctrine, or philosophy. Zen is life itself, lived out fully moment by moment. It is the direct experience of nonduality or wholeness that is completely integrated into everyday life. Nonduality is the experience that you are not separate or isolated from others or from life itself. Since a major portion of my life has been my career as a nurse and a nursing professor, I have included many stories from my nursing practice as examples of Zen and healing. The stories are true, although some of the names and details have been changed to protect the confidentiality of the people involved.

Neither Zen nor healing can be adequately communicated in words. They must be experienced directly. Neither Zen nor healing is a linear process. There are no set stages or phases. Zen realization and healing take place both gradually and in sudden leaps. Both are unpredictable and unfold in unexpected ways. Therefore, this book is not presented in a linear fashion. Rather it is organized around themes that emerge in the practice of Zen and in the experience of healing and wholeness.

Zen stories, sayings, and verses from three classic koan collections—the *Mumonkan,* the *Hekiganroku,* and the *Denkoroku*—are used throughout the book to present Zen insights that can be helpful in the healing process. However, Zen insights are not attainable through reading and the intellect alone. Zen requires actually sitting down and doing it. Therefore, basic instructions for Zen meditation are included at the end of the book and instructions about various aspects of Zen practice are woven throughout the book to invite and encourage readers to try it for themselves.

The image of mountain climbing is often used to describe the process of spiritual development. Initially the seeker is involved in spiritual practice to ascend to the top of the mountain where wisdom and a clear vision of the wholeness of life can be attained. But wisdom and vision are not enough. Further spiritual development lies ahead as the individual matures and descends the mountain to live with wisdom and vision in the details of daily life. In a famous set of Zen ox-herding pictures that depicts the process of spiritual development, the final picture shows a monk returning to town to work in the marketplace like an ordinary person helping those around him.

*Healing Zen* can be used as a guide in ascending the mountain to expand your vision, experience wholeness, and be refreshed. If you are currently struggling with your own health crisis, chronic illness, or efforts with recovery, the essays on Presence, Breathing, Eating, Acceptance, and Balance may be particularly helpful to you. The book also can serve as a guide in descending the mountain to work in the marketplace with healing hands. The experience of wholeness is healing and it frees you to live with beauty, strength, vitality, and compassion. It is my hope that these stories, insights, and teachings will evoke in you a desire to engage in the process of healing yourself and others and will serve as a companion along the way.

I

# DAILY PRACTICE:
# TAKING TIME
# TO HEAL

# WHOLENESS:

## Becoming Aware of Wholeness

The word "heal" comes from an Old English word that means to make whole. Of course we are already whole, so healing involves becoming aware of our wholeness. Healing is more than just being cured of an illness. Even when you cannot be cured, you can experience healing. You can experience wholeness. Healing includes harmony of body, mind, and spirit and an awareness of your oneness with the whole universe.

Healing yourself is also the foundation for healing others. Both the caregiver and the person being cared for can learn and grow with each healing encounter. As you heal both yourself and others you will become increasingly aware of the wholeness of life.

A year ago one of my friends was diagnosed with breast cancer. She had a mastectomy, the cancer was removed, and reconstructive surgery was done. She told me that although her cancer was cured, and she was truly grateful for that, she felt she needed much more healing. She went on a healing journey. She began Zen meditation. Taking time out each day to sit in silence helped her get in touch with new aspects of herself and with the richness of life around her. For many years she had worked long hours as a hospital administrator but now she saw that she needed more time for herself, more time to spend with her family and friends, and more time to be out in nature. She cut back on her work hours and took more vacations. She began reading poetry and took an art class. Gradually she began to feel whole again. In fact she said she began to feel more whole than she had ever felt before.

There is a Zen story that I love to tell. Two young cousins played together as children and were very fond of one another. One cousin was a girl named Seijo, the other a boy named Ochu. When they grew up they fell in love and were heartbroken when Seijo's father selected a different man to be Seijo's husband. Seijo and Ochu ended up running away together to another town to get married and raise a family. After several years, Seijo told her husband how much she missed her family. Ochu said he was homesick also and suggested that they return home and ask her father's forgiveness.

When they reached Seijo's home, Ochu went up to the house first. When he explained what had happened and asked for forgiveness, Seijo's father was astounded. He said that it was impossible because the day Ochu left town, his daughter Seijo became sick and had remained here in the house in bed all these years. Ochu told his father-in-law that this could not be true and that he must come down to the boat, where his daughter and grandchildren were waiting, and see for himself. Just then the homesick Seijo who had been waiting in the boat and the Seijo who had lain ill in bed for many years came walking across the lawn toward each other. The two became one; the divided Seijo was made whole.

This story is, of course, richly symbolic rather than literal. We could say it is about the split that occurs when we are faced with meeting our own needs and following our own dreams and at the same time trying to fulfill the needs and dreams of others. Or perhaps it is about the split or conflict that arises as we try to balance the different types of needs and dreams we each have within us.

This story is also a metaphor for our experience during Zen meditation. When you sit in meditation open to all aspects of yourself, open to all the thoughts and feelings that pass through, you get to know yourself more fully. And in the attitude of openness and acceptance cultivated in meditation, you are free to see and embrace your whole self that is not separate from others, the earth, or the whole universe.

For the past eight years my husband Charles, who is also a Zen teacher, and I have led a local group of people who come together each week for an evening of Zen meditation. This group is called the New River Zen Community.

One summer Jason, the ten-year-old son of one of the women in the New River Zen Community, accidentally hanged himself with a rope while playing in the backyard. He suffered a severe brain injury and was in the hospital for ten months. During Jason's first two weeks in the hospital, his mother, Fran, had several friends take turns helping her care for him at night so she could remain at his bedside and still get some sleep. During the night when I helped out, I sat beside the bed, listened to Jason's breathing, and repositioned his head when he had trouble clearing his airway. I kept him clean and dry. When he became restless and agitated, I held his hand, talked to him reassuringly, and protected him from pulling out any tubes or hurting himself. In the morning we gave him a bath, shampooed his hair, and dressed him in a clean hospital gown and high-top Nikes.

Caring for Jason I recalled Huston Smith's statement that from a Buddhist perspective, "We become compassionate not from altruism which denies the self for the sake of other, but from the insight that sees and feels one is the other." My Zen practice helps me experience myself and the world in this way. As I positioned Jason's arms and legs, it was my own arms and legs that I moved. As I shampooed his hair, it was my own hair that I washed. As I laced and tied his shoes, I laced and tied my own shoes. As his mother slept in anguish at his bedside, I slept in anguish also.

As I shared the experience of caring for Jason with his family, I learned so much. They are of Greek and Italian descent and are much more expressive and full of life than I tend to be. They shared their grief openly with large numbers of family and friends who visited the hospital in a steady stream, bringing flowers, balloons, food, and prayers. I learned how it feels to be more connected to people in good times and bad, in sorrow and joy, not separate and isolated. Jason's grandmother brought some of her homemade wine to the hospital and as Fran passed the bottle around before going to bed one night she said, "This is our communion."

When Jason came home, he still could not move any of his extremities or speak. Three times a day for an hour and a half many volunteers helped his family do patterning with him as part of his rehabilitation program. We repetitively moved his head, arms, and legs through the motions of crawling. While we did this, we sang silly songs because they made him laugh and relax instead of cry and get agitated. I usually moved the left leg because it was most contracted and difficult to move. I learned that when you move one leg of one little boy unable to move it for himself, the whole universe moves.

From the perspective of wholeness, no part is separate from the whole and each part contains the whole. When the part moves, the whole moves. The direct experience of this oneness and unity of life gives the caregiver the energy and strength to reach out to heal others.

In the fall Jason died. There is nothing sadder than the death of a child. One evening in October when New River Zen Community was outside doing walking meditation between sitting meditation periods, the line of meditators stopped halfway up the hill. Jason's mother and father each took a handful of Jason's ashes and in silence scattered them on the hillside. It was a cool moonlit night and the ashes swirled in the breeze like incense rising. After a few moments we continued to walk silently up the hill, our hearts broken open to life, death, the surrounding mountains, the night sky, and the whole universe.

Although Jason's accident and death were tragic, his parents faced it head on with all their resources. They did not withdraw or deny what was happening. They did not isolate themselves in their sorrow, but rather accepted with gratitude the support and assistance of family, friends, and strangers from near and far. They remained open to and united with the great mysteries of life. When we open ourselves in times of illness, loss, sorrow, or pain, we remain open to the possibilities for healing.

# PRESENCE:

## *Being Present to Yourself*
## *and Others*

So often we are daydreaming, preoccupied, or running off in all directions and we miss what is happening right in front of our eyes. We miss our own precious lives. When we are wholly present, we are wholly alive.

Presence is the essence of the healing process. As you are present to more and more of yourself and more and more of your life, you become increasingly aware of your wholeness. Getting to know, acknowledge, and accept without judging, the many facets of yourself is healing. When you are fully present to yourself and your life, you can also reach out in wholeness and be fully present in body, mind, and spirit to another who is in need of healing.

In my work as a nurse, the healing effect of physical presence is very apparent. Especially when a person is critically ill, the physical presence of the nurse to constantly monitor the rapidly changing condition of the patient is essential. In addition to the hands-on skills that are used to keep the patient alive, the physical presence of the nurse and the way he or she touches the patient, can have a healing effect.

I have often seen the physical presence and assistance of a trusted family member or friend relieve a patient's anxiety and provide the comfort he or she needed to rest and heal more quickly. One night when my father was in the hospital after having a stroke, I spent the night sleeping on a cot beside his bed. This way he didn't have to be tied down in bed and could get a better night's rest. Off and on throughout the night he stirred restlessly and called out for help. Each time I said, "I'm right here, Dad. What do you need?" He would say, "Nothing." Reassured that I was nearby if he needed anything, he would roll over and fall back to sleep.

The night I spent in the hospital with my father reminded me of a well-known Zen story about an esteemed old Zen master who called out three times to a young monk who was assigned to be his attendant. Each time the master called out "Attendant!" Each time, without hesitation, the monk walked swiftly to his master's side and said, "Yes!" The old master could hear in the monk's brisk footsteps across the wooden floor and in his wholehearted "Yes!" that he was fully present and ready to help. The master greatly praised the monk's enlightenment. The young monk did not hesitate or sigh when he heard the second or third call. Each time he responded as if it were the very first call. He was fully present here and now. He was not just physically present, he was attentive and not otherwise preoccupied or distracted.

Physical presence can be very comforting, but physical presence alone is not enough. Perhaps the most healing thing one person can do for another is to listen. One of my friends is an oncology nurse. Last year, she took care of a middle-aged man with lung cancer who was undergoing chemotherapy. He was single and lived several hundred miles from his family. He said his coworkers and friends didn't seem to want to talk about a difficult topic like cancer. Each time he came for a chemotherapy treatment he spoke openly with my friend about whatever was on his mind. She listened attentively without being judgmental about what he shared. They developed a close relationship with one another. Fortunately, the chemotherapy was effective and his cancer was cured. Several months later she received a thank-you card from him. He thanked her for being there with him in his darkest hour and he said he didn't know how he would have made it through the ordeal without her listening ear and warm heart. She was not only physically present with him, but she was also present in mind and spirit.

Zen meditation helps us wake up and be fully present—body, mind, and spirit—right here and now. Zen meditation can be thought of as a way of practicing being present. You sit in silence, awake and open to the present moment. It is an opportunity to slow down, become aware of your breathing, and take a break from your usual thoughts and preoccupations. Sitting in meditation before you start your day, you hear the beauty of the first birdsong, hear the rhythm of the water running as others take their showers, and see the light of dawn gradually brighten. You become more sensitive and alive.

Lisa, a social worker, started meditating recently and at first she didn't think she would be able to sit still for any longer than five minutes because she is such an active person. But when she actually tried it she was amazed by all there was to hear and see and feel, the patterns of light and shadow reflected through the window onto the floor, a cool breeze across her cheek, the sensation of her belly gently rising and falling, and the sound of passing cars. Her body and mind enjoyed the time away from her usual business. One day after several months of meditating each morning she commented that she noticed a change in the quality of her ability to be truly present with her clients. Although she had always tried to listen carefully to what they were saying, now she felt more fully present in body and mind.

The sense of presence experienced during the regular daily practice of meditation overflows into the rest of your life and you learn to be fully present in each moment throughout the day. Each moment, person, and blade of grass contains the whole. When you are fully awake and present, you are present with the whole self that is not separate from the whole universe. When you are wholly present, you transcend the boundaries of self and other, of time and space. You transcend the boundaries of life and death.

For several months, I was the primary nurse for a tiny baby who was fourteen weeks premature. The baby's parents lived on a farm more than a hundred miles from the medical center. The parents and I developed a close relationship as we lived day by day, minute by minute, sharing their daughter's ups and downs. Three or four times a week they visited the neonatal intensive care unit and in between, we talked with each other on the phone. One day the baby took a sudden turn for the worse and died before her parents could get to the medical center.

While we were waiting for the parents to arrive, I bathed the baby, dressed her in one of the fancy nighties her mother had bought for her, wrapped her in a pink receiving blanket, and held her in my arms, rocking her in one of the big rocking chairs on the unit.

When her parents arrived, they took turns holding and rocking their daughter as tears streamed down their faces. They thanked me for being with them while they said good-bye to her. They said it meant so much to them to know that their baby was not alone while they were driving there that day. They knew that I was present with her while she was dying and that even after she was dead I would be with her until they could get there. The baby's parents and I lingered there together in her presence, recalling the moments of her short life.

There is a Zen verse that urges us to be wholly present to each moment of life.

> *Lightning flashing,*
> *Sparks shooting from a flint;*
> *A moment's blinking . . .*
> *It's already missed.*

If you are not awake and present you miss life as it flashes right in front of you. Being present to life, you are able to be present to death as well. Being present to the people in your life and to all that surrounds you, you don't miss the uniqueness of each creation. Being present you clearly see the spark, vitality, and preciousness of life. Presence is life itself.

# BREATHING:

## *Living Life One Breath at a Time*

Breathing is essential to life. If a person stops breathing you immediately start CPR. You clear the airway and provide mouth-to-mouth resuscitation if necessary. Several times when I've stopped to provide first aid at the scene of an accident, the injured people were so upset that they were either holding their breath or hyperventilating. I had them take a few slow deep breaths to calm down while I checked them over for bleeding. The slow breaths helped them remain calm and still while waiting for the rescue squad to arrive.

Anytime you are feeling anxious a few slow deep breaths will help you relax. When you're feeling very angry a few slow deep breaths will help you regain your equanimity. Breathing can even ease the pain of childbirth. The breath is a wonderful friend who is with you all the time and can help you cope with many difficult situations.

Not only can you work with the breath on the physical and psychological levels, but you can also work with it on the spiritual level. When you are aware of your breathing you experience your interdependence with the environment around you. We are dependent upon clean air and we share the air with those around us. Breathing unites us with all of creation. When we breathe, we breathe with all of nature, with all the people, animals, and plants on the earth. The direct experience of this unity is a moving spiritual experience.

Often I have cared for people who were hovering between life and death. One elderly man I took care of at the time of his death had suffered several strokes and was very debilitated. The day before he died, he lapsed into unconsciousness. It was the wish of the family, and considered best by the health care team, that the man be kept as comfortable as possible and be allowed to die. He lay in bed breathing very rapidly and shallowly hour after hour. His airway was clear and he did not struggle or seem to be uncomfortable so his family sat by his bedside holding his hands and watching him breathe. A few times he stopped breathing briefly and then started up again. Then he stopped breathing and didn't start up again. The family felt that it was healing for them to be allowed to be with him as he breathed his last breaths and to see that he died peacefully.

Life begins and ends with the breath. When my daughter Clare was born she was a big eight-and-a-half-pound baby. The doctor held her up and said, "She's a beautiful baby girl!" Because the delivery was long and hard, I was weak and confused and Clare was quite blue. I looked at Clare and with great concern and urgency said, "She's not breathing." The doctor brought her up closer to me and said, "No Ellen, she's all right. She's breathing." Clare began to move her arms and legs, she let out a wonderful cry, and she turned pink before my eyes. Every breath is a miracle.

There is a Zen story about how a single breath can free us from the confines of our intellectualizing and unite us with all creation. Tokusan was a brilliant scripture scholar who went to study with Zen Master Ryutan. One night as Tokusan was leaving to go home to bed after a long evening of discussion, he noticed that it was pitch black outside. Zen Master Ryutan lit a lantern and handed it to Tokusan. Just as Tokusan reached for the lantern, Ryutan blew it out. In that moment, Tokusan experienced enlightenment and bowed in gratitude. Tokusan realized that he was not dependent upon words and teachings to light the way for him. Even in times of darkness, he could experience his essential nature directly and be a lamp unto himself.

With a single puff of air from the Zen master's mouth, Tokusan saw what he had not been able to see up until then. All of his scripture study and discussion had not communicated what a single breath of air communicated to him. Tokusan directly experienced that awakening is not dependent on intellectual grasping. The next day Tokusan gathered all of his commentaries on the scriptures into a huge pile and burned them. He told the group assembled there that intellectual speculation is like grasping at straws and can't compare to the vastness of direct experience. The direct experience of a single breath unites us with all creation.

Tokusan's burning of the manuscripts was rather dramatic, but the point he was making was an important one so perhaps it warranted a bit of drama. There is great value to intellectual pursuits, scripture, and study, but we must not allow them to limit us or cut us off from direct experience of the whole. Thoughts and words can become blinders and barriers that keep us from experiencing life itself. Words can't blow out a lantern. With a simple puff of air, the flame goes out.

Having a serious illness cuts through your usual mode of operating and thinking about life. Your normal routine comes to a halt and you experience that things are not going to continue as you planned and expected. You are forced to let go of your plans and expectations. Healing begins when you start living life one breath at a time.

Joni was an eight-year-old little girl with cystic fibrosis who taught me to live life one breath at a time and to appreciate that each breath is precious. Joni got frequent respiratory infections and each time she came into the hospital she had a very involved routine of medications and treatments to help clear her lungs so she could breathe. Each day we vibrated her chest while she lay in various positions in order to loosen and remove the secretions that blocked the air from entering her lungs. Even though she was very thin, pale, and frail she got so much enjoyment out of life. She had a huge collection of postcards from all over the country and around the world that family and friends had sent her. Almost daily she got a new postcard in the mail and each time she was thoroughly excited and pleased. She amused herself for end-less hours arranging, rearranging, and telling stories about her cards. Joni's favorite times were when her friends, cousins, or other kids on the unit came to visit her. These visits always erupted into fits of giggling. Even though Joni struggled every day just to breathe, she was full of life and shared her liveliness with everyone who came in contact with her. She not only made you aware of how lucky you were to be able to breathe, she made you feel glad to be alive.

If we live our lives with gratitude for each breath, life is rich and full. Each breath is a gift to be enjoyed and shared. Each breath is breathed in the present moment. An awareness of the breath draws us into experiencing the fluidity of the present moment. We are free to open the windows and take a breath of fresh air. We are free to work to preserve the environment so all life will have fresh air to breathe. With each breath we can see that life is just this breath!

The breath is an important aspect of Zen meditation. The posture you sit in during meditation encourages re-laxed, natural breathing. Your back is straight, your shoulders are back slightly, and your pelvis is tilted for-ward a little. In this position the chest is free to expand and the abdomen can move in and out freely.

You don't try to regulate your breathing in any way. Zen meditation is not like yogic techniques, which are aimed at regulating the breath. You simply allow natural breathing to take place. During meditation you may notice that your breath becomes slow, deep, calm, and regular. But you don't try for this. It happens naturally as you settle down in the silence and stillness of meditation.

Many people have difficulty with restlessness when they first begin Zen meditation. For some people it is a great help to count the breath. One practice is to count each exhalation up to ten and then start over with one. The first exhalation is one, the second exhalation is two, the third exhalation is three, and so forth up to ten. When you find that you have drifted off into thought, you simply come back to your breath and start counting again with the number one. Some people find that it takes several weeks of practice to get beyond three or four. But eventually your mind and body get used to settling down and it is easy to get to ten most of the time.

After counting the breath comes easily, the counting can be dropped and you can just be aware of the breath. When you are paying attention to the breath it is best that your attention be in your belly. Attending to your breath in your belly gets you out of your head and into your body. This helps you get away from the habitual tendency to think and intellectualize. When you become aware that you have drifted off into thought, you simply bring your attention back to your breath.

Later you can progress to just sitting. During the practice of just sitting, when you become aware that you have drifted off into thought you simply bring your attention back to just sitting right here and now. Although counting the breath and attending to the breath are good beginning practices, they are also useful to come back to from time to time no matter how many years a person has been practicing. These are good basic practices that settle, strengthen, energize, and open us.

When you are awake and aware you experience that you are one with the breath. There is no separation between your breath and the breath of all creation. It ceaselessly circles through all creation and you are free to move with it. You are the breath.

# ENERGY:

## *Living with Vitality*

Most people equate energy, vitality, and enthusiasm for life with excellent health. Many people who have an acute or chronic illness find fatigue, tiredness, decreased energy, weakness, and exhaustion to be some of their most troubling and debilitating symptoms.

Fatigue can have many causes. It may result from medical disorders, the side effects of medication, stress, depression, poor nutrition, lack of sleep, or lack of physical fitness. The first step in dealing with fatigue is to seek treatment for any medical problems you may have and get your medications adjusted to minimize the side effects. Beyond that, eating nourishing food, getting a good night's sleep, exercising regularly, and taking naps may be helpful. Meditation is useful in relieving fatigue that is caused by stress. In addition to being physically relaxing, it calms your mind. At the same time, it refreshes and enlivens your body and mind. Meditation renews your spirit and has an energizing effect.

Recently a friend had cancer that required major surgery. Right after surgery she felt so weak that she didn't have the energy to speak or even to lift her head off the pillow. During the first few days of her recovery, she was unable to take a shower or comb her hair. Little by little, as healing took place her energy began to return and she could enjoy walking around on the unit, visiting with friends, and reading a good book. Over the next several months she ate nutritious food, got plenty of rest, and gradually resumed her routine of walking two miles four times a week.

She had been meditating for several years prior to her surgery. The first couple of days after surgery, she was too weak to meditate. By the third day she meditated for a short period lying with the head of her bed slightly raised and she found that it relaxed her. For several days she continued to meditate while lying in bed. Over the next few weeks she gradually resumed her usual meditation practice, at first sitting on a chair and later on her meditation mat and cushion.

Both energy and tiredness are aspects of the whole. Zen practice helps you accept the human condition and the circumstances of life just as they are. You cannot expect to be energetic all the time. Sometimes you become tired and must rest. When you rest, lie down and thoroughly enjoy resting. One Zen master in ancient China expressed it this way:

> *I stretch out both legs and take a long nap;*
> *And here there is neither true nor false.*
> *Truly, such is the essence of the Way.*

When I think of energy, I think of Roshi Richardson. She is in her seventies and has survived cancer and hip replacement surgery. She is very active teaching Zen most mornings and many evenings at Clare Sangha in Baltimore. She often travels around the country to lead Zen retreats. In between she says she spends her time doing the laundry, cooking, doing the dishes, recycling, and taking out the trash. Most summer afternoons, she swims laps in the pool. Afterwards she rests with great zest, sunning on a chaise longue. Most impressive of all is the warmth and energy in her eyes and in her voice as she listens and speaks, giving her total attention to each person she meets.

In recent years more and more people have become interested in various forms of energy medicine. Some people understand energy medicine as a process whereby the healer gives energy to the person in need of healing. From a Zen perspective energy is not viewed as a commodity or thing that can be given or received. Your energy is not separate from the energy of the whole universe. You are not separate from the whole. A healer helps you stop building walls and barriers within yourself and between yourself and the world. Letting down the walls and barriers that block the flow of energy allows you to experience wholeness and healing.

Many years ago when Zen Master Mumon gave instructions to the monks on how to meditate, he told them to exhaust every ounce of energy they had in doing it. When you are sitting in Zen meditation, you are not just sitting there. You are not daydreaming or fantasizing. All of your energy is used to be awake and present in the moment. Sometimes at Zen retreats a meditator will come in to see me for individual instruction and say, "Nothing is happening. I'm just sitting there." Often I respond by telling the person, "Bring more energy to your practice. Don't just sit there. Don't just be aware in your head. Bring your awareness down into your belly. Be one with your breath deep down in your belly. Wake up, sit up, pay attention, and be fully present with every cell in your body." It takes energy to sit like this, but it is also energizing.

Although you bring all your energy to the practice of Zen meditation, you don't strain. You don't strive for some predetermined goal. You simply bring all your energy and attention to being right here in the present moment just as it is. You don't dissipate your energy by intentionally thinking about the past, planning for the future, or wishing things were different than they are. Thoughts and feelings do come and go while you are sitting, but you neither add to them nor try to push them away. You simply bring your attention back to sitting in the present moment, letting thoughts and feelings come and go as they will. When your energy is not dissipated by adding to thought or by trying to push thought away, it is available to be awake, alive, and fully present.

One day a monk asked Zen Master Kyorin, "What is the essence of Zen?" Zen Master Kyorin said, "Sitting long and getting tired." In his reply Zen Master Kyorin presented the fact of Zen practice. When we sit, we sit and when we are tired, we are tired.

Zen meditation takes both physical and mental energy. When Buddha first set out seeking enlightenment, he engaged in ascetic practices such as fasting and not sleeping. However, he nearly died from such austerities and he found he did not have the energy to meditate. Buddha came to see the value of moderation and later practiced and taught his disciples to follow the middle way between indulgence and asceticism.

During weeklong intensive Zen retreats participants often experience tiredness, but at the same time, they expand their vision and see themselves and the world in a new way. This is exciting, exhilarating, and energizing. Zen is not just tiredness; it is also vitality and enthusiasm. The vitality and enthusiasm cultivated by Zen practice is apparent when a Zen teacher gives a talk. A Zen talk is not just a lecture. It is a lively presentation of the essence of Zen. Rather than a dry philosophical discourse, it is dramatic, energetic, and evocative.

As you sit in meditation with energy, enthusiasm, and attentiveness you gain an awareness of subtler forms of energy. Sitting in silence and stillness you become aware of subtle energy in the body and of the way you block the flow of energy. You may notice that you are blocking the flow of energy by constricting your breathing. When you see this you can stop constricting your breath, begin breathing naturally, and allow the flow of energy. Or perhaps you are blocking the flow of energy through the body by the way you defend yourself from painful experiences and emotions. Sitting in meditation you see that you are free to let down your defenses. You can allow the energy used in maintaining your defenses to flow freely and be available to enjoy the beauty of life and to deal with adversity.

Although it takes energy to practice meditation, it increases your energy. When you sit in meditation, aware and open, you experience that there is no separation between your own energy field and the energy of the whole universe. This greatly expands your energy resources. During times of illness you can lay in bed resting and meditating, open to the energy of the universe. With patience, good medical care, wholesome food, and appropriate exercise, gradually you will heal and regain your usual strength. Even if a physical cure does not occur, meditation will lift your spirits and help you rest peacefully. Energy is also important in the life of a caregiver. The increased energy from meditating is not only healing for yourself, it is useful in caring for others. Often caregiving is demanding both physically and emotionally. When you feel tired, rundown, and overwhelmed, you can't be as effective in healing others as you would like to be. Meditation helps you learn how to manage your energy so you can be healing to both yourself and others.

# CONFIDENCE:

## *Having Confidence in Yourself and Trust in Others*

An attitude of confidence helps you face the challenges of life and ride out times of adversity. Although feelings of fear, anxiety, discouragement, and doubt are a natural part of being human, if you don't also have confidence and trust, these feelings can become excessive and paralyze you. Being confident in yourself, in your own experience of life, and in your ability to learn and grow, leads to self-healing and allows you to help others have the confidence and trust they need to heal.

When I was in the hospital after having a hysterectomy, I needed a blood transfusion. A young nurse, who had been one of my students the year before, was taking care of me that evening. As she hung the unit of blood on the IV pole next to my bed, she said, "This is my first blood transfusion, but I can do this. I just took an in-service class on administering blood this week. My clinical leader will stand by and watch in case I need help." I admired this young nurse's confidence in herself and her sense of excitement as she expanded her skills.

At the first Zen retreat Roshi Kennedy led after becoming a Zen teacher, he urged those of us attending the retreat to sit in meditation with confidence. He commented on how many people in our society are depressed these days and he said, "Don't sit with depression. Sit with joy. Sit with confidence." In Zen meditation you sit up straight and take a good look at what is right in front of your eyes.

There is a Zen verse that clearly points us in the direction of self-confidence:

> *Don't draw another's bow;*
> *Don't ride another's horse;*
> *Don't speak of another's faults;*
> *Don't try to know another's affairs.*

The point of Zen practice is to see for yourself, to experience directly. Regardless of what another is experiencing, you need to experience for yourself. Paying attention to another's faults or affairs is just a distraction from paying attention to what is happening right here and now. A Zen teacher won't ask you about what another is doing or seeing. The Zen teacher will ask you, "How do *you* see it?"

This verse also helps you move beyond the duality of self and other to the direct experience of nonduality or wholeness. From the perspective of the whole, or the underlying unity of all things, there is no self and other. There is only one self. From this perspective, there are no limits to your self-confidence.

Confidence in yourself leads to trusting others. To persist in sitting period after period of meditation requires trust. You need to have confidence and trust that there is something valuable to be seen. This can be viewed as trust in the long tradition of Zen teachers going back to Buddha himself. It is trust that Buddha did indeed have a direct experience of nonduality or wholeness and that this insight relieves the suffering of humanity. It is trust that sitting in meditation is an effective way for an individual to have the direct experience of nonduality or wholeness for him or herself.

Your defenses protect you from anxiety, conflict, discomfort, and pain, but they also wall you off from experiencing the whole. Letting down your defenses requires trust. You need a deep level of trust that the experience of not existing as a separate self will be a good experience. You need to trust that experiencing wholeness will be more satisfying than holding on to the familiar experience of fragmentation. You need trust and openness in order to see things differently and to have a vast new experience.

Before you can trust you must first get to know and acknowledge your fears and anxieties. I once saw a Zen calligraphy of an iron bar. The caption that accompanied the picture said that if you don't fear the iron bar you will face grave consequences in hell. We cannot deny that we live in a world of cause and effect and that fear and anxiety are very real aspects of our human existence.

Sitting in meditation day after day you get to know your fears and anxieties intimately. You see them arise in the body and mind, over and over again. At the same time that you are getting to know and acknowledge your fears and anxieties, you are also opening to something larger. You see that your fears and anxieties are aspects of the whole. Your fears and anxieties remain, but they lose their grip on your total existence; they cease to constrict your vision. You gain the flexibility to be both fearful and not fearful, both anxious and in touch with something larger than your anxiety.

Some people experience great fear when they realize their interdependence with everything else in the world. They see themselves as fiercely independent and are frightened to acknowledge that there is much that is beyond their control. At the same time, they can find this realization liberating, freeing them from the need to try to control all aspects of life. In some ways it's like learning to swim. Rather than being paralyzed by the fear of drowning, the swimmer lets go and relaxes, allowing the water to support the body. The swimmer learns to move the arms and legs just enough to stay afloat and propel the body through the water.

Often in order to heal you must accept your vulnerability and be willing to trust others. Every person undergoing surgery is completely vulnerable as they lose consciousness during anesthesia. The patient is totally dependent on the team of doctors and nurses performing the procedures and caring for them afterward. In addition, they are dependent on all of the people who manufacture, clean, and maintain the medical equipment and supplies that are used in their care. Undergoing surgery is a direct experience of interdependence and the trust required to heal.

As human beings we are interdependent, vulnerable, and imperfect. The realization of these aspects of our shared humanity gives us the confidence to try new experiences even though we may make a mistake. The chairperson of a nursing department where I work once said, "Anyone who never makes any mistakes probably isn't doing anything." I like working for someone who sees things this way because it gives me the confidence and freedom to do my work creatively, the way I think best. When I make a mistake, I learn from the mistake and move on with confidence to try again. When we feel free to allow our faults to show to ourselves and others, we are more authentic, whole human beings.

The first time Roshi Kennedy asked me to give a Zen talk at a retreat he was leading in California, I carefully prepared and typed the talk beforehand. In the airport on the way to the retreat, I asked him if he wanted to look over what I planned to say. He declined and said that whatever I had to say was okay with him. Then a broad smile came over his face and he said, "See what confidence I have in you?" He taught me that Zen is "nothing but trusting the Self."

Confidence and trust in yourself and others are necessary in order to allow yourself to relax and heal yourself. They provide the footing from which you can dare to step out to try to help others heal.

# BEING GROUNDED:

*Staying Rooted in the Earth and
Practical Activities of Life*

Being rooted in the earth and the practical everyday activities of life is healing. When you are grounded you
don't feel alienated or out of touch. Being aware of the
great earth that sustains you and of everyday activities
like eating, washing the dishes, and going to work helps
you feel connected to the world around you and to the
rhythm of life.

One of the most healing areas in the psychiatric hospital, where I take the student nurses for clinical learning
experiences, is the horticulture therapy greenhouse. Often a person with Alzheimer's disease, or a person recovering from psychosis or depression, will come back to life
before my eyes as they dig in the earth, crumble clods of
dirt with their hands, transplant seedlings, and carefully
water them.

One eighty-seven-year-old man, living in a nearby
retirement home, keeps a beautiful rose garden in the
courtyard. Every morning he is out tending his roses and
welcoming the sun as it comes up. The huge red, pink,
and yellow blossoms bring color and beauty into his life
and the lives of the other residents of the home, many of
whom are no longer able to garden. He says his garden
keeps him in touch with the earth and new life. Being
grounded in this way enables him to reach out to others.

He cuts the roses, arranges them in beautiful bouquets, and gives them to the residents who are ill. Being grounded helps to heal yourself and others.

Zen practice is grounded. It's not abstract or ethereal. It's rooted like a great tree and yet it moves like electricity seeking ground. In the posture you assume for Zen meditation, you are seated with the bottom and two knees on the ground. Sitting on a bench, the bottom is on the bench and the two knees, lower legs, and feet are firmly on the ground. In a chair you are in contact with the front of the chair and both feet are planted flat on the ground. These postures ground you.

When we sit for more than one twenty-five-minute period of meditation consecutively, we do five or ten minutes of walking meditation between the periods of sitting meditation. We line up in a row behind the person leading the walking meditation and walk along about two feet behind the person in front of us like one long caterpillar. As we walk our attention is on the feeling of our feet coming in contact with the ground, one foot after the other. When possible, we do walking meditation outdoors where the earth and all of nature help to ground us.

In both walking and sitting meditation, your eyes are open and cast down on the ground about three feet in front of you. You don't close your eyes and drift off into some dream world. You remain right here in contact with whatever is right in front of you.

Several years ago, Roshi Niklaus Brantschen, a Zen teacher from Switzerland, visited us in Virginia. While we were hiking to a high cliff in the nearby Appalachian Mountains called Barney's Wall, he told us about his early years as a guide taking climbers up the Matterhorn. He instructed us that it's important to keep three points touching the ground at all times while mountain climbing. You move one limb at a time while maintaining contact with the other three. You have to be well grounded to climb high.

Sometimes the path of Zen has been called "going straight up the mountain." On the spiritual path, as well as the mountain trail, a traveler can fall or get lost if not properly grounded. To remain grounded, you use your common sense, you meet the basic needs of yourself and others, and you are practical.

In his "Mountains and Water Sutra" Zen Master Dogen speaks about mountains standing and also about mountains flowing. Even the mountains, which stand for thousands of years and seem not to change, are changing. Yet at the same time they are a manifestation of the unchanging essential nature of reality. Mountains are flowing and not flowing.

There is a Zen koan, or question that cannot be answered with the intellect alone, that asks, "How does a mountain walk?" Zen practice teaches you how to sit grounded like a great mountain, and at the same time you also learn how to walk, flow, and even dance like a mountain.

New River Zen Community was named after the New River that flows through the region where we live.

Geologists have determined that the New River is the second oldest river in the world, second only to the Nile. So it seemed appropriate to name a Zen community after a river that is both very old and entirely new each moment. A favorite pastime on a hot summer day is to go over to McCoy and float down a section of the New River in an inner tube. Floating down the river in a tube, you can clearly see the mountains flowing by.

There is a Zen story that clearly expresses the quality of being grounded. A monk entered the monastery and begged Zen Master Joshu for instruction. Joshu asked, "Have you eaten your rice gruel yet?" The monk replied, "Yes, I have." Joshu responded, "Then wash your bowls."

In asking, "Have you eaten your rice gruel yet?" Joshu was asking the monk if he had realized or glimpsed his essential nature yet. When the monk answered that he had, Joshu immediately moved him along to the next step, which was to actualize this insight in his everyday actions. In a practical, everyday action like washing the dishes, our essential nature is manifested.

There is nothing lofty and elevated here. The mundane is seen as magnificent. The imagery used by Joshu grounds us in our daily life and basic human needs. The eating of rice gruel represents seeing essential nature. We must eat to survive. In the East the staple is rice, in the West wheat, and for the Native Americans corn. All of these are planted in the earth, watered, cultivated, harvested, and eaten and they become our body. In the Christian tradition, the bread is the body of Christ. In

Native-American cultures corn is the body of Corn Mother. In Zen terms we can say that a handful of rice is the Buddha.

Wheat is ground into flour. Corn is ground into meal. Rice is sifted to remove the hulls. These are refining processes. Meditating day after day on a regular basis can be viewed as a refining process. The back and forth movement of grinding and sifting is like the back and forth movement between meditation and action, realization and actualization.

Marilou Awiatka, a Cherokee/Appalachian writer, says that in the West, we have looked vertically to heaven to know our Father, but we are not grounded in the earth. We do not know our Mother the corn spirit, Selu. She suggests that if we knew our Mother who grows in the ground, we would take better care of the earth. At Radford University where I teach nursing, there is a nature conservancy and retreat center called Selu Conservancy. In the center of the retreat building, there is a beautiful semisubterranean seven-sided Cherokee-style meeting room. In the floor of the room is a mosaic of a corn plant in honor of Selu. The room has a healing effect as you sit within mother earth grounded in the reality that she constantly sustains and nourishes us.

When you are in need of healing, reconnecting with the earth is often helpful. In addition, it helps to return to the simple activities of daily living, like walking, bathing, dressing, and cooking, as soon as your condition permits. This way you stay in touch with the earth and with the flow of life. Staying in touch with the earth and the manual tasks of caregiving also helps ground the caregiver and keep him or her from becoming overwhelmed by the complexity and stress of the caregiving role. With your feet on the ground you are better able to maintain your own health and have the stability to promote the healing of others.

# BEING NATURAL:

## *Discovering Natural Beauty*

Reconnecting with nature is healing for body, mind, and spirit. Reconnecting with nature helps you see that you extend beyond your skin and that you are the air you breathe. You are the water you drink. You are the soil in which your food is grown. You are not separate and isolated. You are interdependent with all the plants, the animals, the earth, and the sky.

In the natural environment you can rediscover your own natural beauty. There is no need to maintain a facade or false image. You can be yourself and breathe freely. For many people being outdoors surrounded by nature is a form of relaxation, meditation, and worship. The beauty of nature awakens and nourishes you spiritually.

One of the psychiatric hospitals where I take students for clinical experience recognizes the healing effect of nature and maintains beautiful walking trails and gardens on the hospital grounds. Each day the patients and staff go outside together for long walks. This is a time of healing for both patients and staff.

A middle-aged man with bipolar disorder who has been a patient at the hospital off and on for many years has a little poodle. Each time the man is discharged, the little dog comes along in the car with his parents to pick him up. The dog always greets him with great enthusiasm jumping up onto his lap and licking his cheeks. Once when the man required a long hospitalization, the psychiatrist allowed the dog to stay in the hospital. The dog walked proudly up and down the hallway with a blue plastic armband on his front right leg. The dog calmed the patient and helped him to feel loved and connected. Human beings need to feel connected with the natural world of plants and animals. Animals are spontaneous and nonjudgmental and they bring out these qualities in us.

Zen practice cultivates an appreciation for the natural environment. Sitting in meditation helps you slow down enough to take a good look at the incredible beauty that surrounds you with each changing season. My husband Charles and I live in the feminine flowering mountains of the southeast. Spring greets us with purple redbud trees and clouds of white dogwoods scattered throughout the forest. During walking meditations on summer evenings the air is full of the sweet scent of honeysuckle.

Our friends Sarah and Jim have an organic blueberry farm in the mountains nearby. During the summer months, people go to the farm to pick their own blueberries. They are the plumpest, bluest, sweetest blueberries I have ever eaten. Each is a miracle and is naturally nourishing to body, mind, and spirit.

The beauty of the world around us cannot be fully expressed in words, pictures, or movies. It must be experienced firsthand. There is a line from a Zen verse that emphasizes the importance of direct experience:

*The vermilion boat so beautiful that no painting*
*can do it justice.*

This line reminds me of the time Charles and I camped at
the base of the Vermilion Cliffs in Arizona. What color is
vermilion? I discovered that it is a hundred shades of red
as the sun set and rose again the next morning. During
the night it snowed and the white of the snow made the
red of the cliffs even redder against a sky that was so crisp
and clear it was navy blue. Words cannot express the
clarity, vastness, and sense of nonseparation we experienced that morning at the cliffs.

Zen does not stop with a greater appreciation of nature. Sometimes nature is the trigger for a deep awakening to your true nature which is the true nature of
everything. Zen Master Ling-yun's awakening was triggered by peach blossoms. His experience is expressed in
the verse:

*The red of the rustic village is unknown*
*to the peach blossoms;*
*Yet, they instruct Ling-yun to arrive*
*at doubtlessness.*

Although the peach blossom did not teach Ling-yun anything in words, their sheer beauty triggered in him a direct experience of his true nature, thereby erasing all
doubt from his mind. For others the trigger was the
sound of a pebble striking bamboo, a star, a bird song, or
a mountain range.

In the direct experience of your true nature, which is also called your essential or original nature, you realize that you are not separate from the world around you. You see that you are essentially beautiful just the way you are. Your essential or original nature, just like that of a newborn baby, has a natural beauty all its own.

While working as a nurse in the neonatal intensive care unit, I often went to the delivery room for high-risk births. If a baby was born with a problem, I was ready to immediately transfer him or her to the intensive care nursery. One day while I was standing by in the delivery room, a baby was born with ambiguous genitalia. We could not tell if the baby was a boy or girl. The doctor delivering the baby was wise and compassionate. He did not miss a beat. Instead of the usual, "It's a boy" or "It's a girl" he said, "It's a beautiful baby." He placed the baby in the mother's arms and then went on to explain the situation and what would need to be done later on. The baby was beautiful with soft pink skin, bright alert eyes, and arms and legs moving freely and spontaneously. Every baby is naturally beautiful. Even if the baby doesn't look like the Gerber baby, each is so fresh and new that the original nature shines through and can be easily seen and felt.

Regardless of physical characteristics or psychological problems, each person's original nature is beautiful. The natural beauty and original nature of a baby is not difficult to see, but often it's harder to see with adults.

Sometimes it's most difficult of all to see your own natural beauty, just as you are. Often your friends can see it easier than you can. A friend is someone you can be natural with. With a friend you feel free to be just as you are. You can be as fresh and new and natural as a baby.

When you realize your true nature, you realize you are nature. In describing his awakening to his true nature, Yamada Roshi quoted Zen Master Dogen, "I came to realize clearly that Mind is no other than mountains and rivers and the great wide earth, the sun and the moon and the stars." When your unity with nature is a direct experience, you relate differently to the earth and the sky. Your realization is actualized in action to conserve natural resources and to preserve the natural beauty of the planet.

Zen practice is ecological. When you come together to meditate, or when you meditate on your own at home, you don't consume much. Aside from a mat and a cushion and perhaps a candle or a stick of incense, you don't need a lot of fancy equipment or supplies. You spend a pleasant day or evening together and at the same time conserve the natural environment.

The process of doing Zen meditation is natural. You sit and you breathe. You don't control your breath in any way. You just breathe naturally. During meditation you are not trying to create any image, feeling, or experience. You are just sitting attentively noticing what naturally occurs. When your mind wanders off in chatter, you come back to just sitting naturally in the present moment.

In the process of returning to the present moment, you let go of your habitual, conditioned thoughts and your mind naturally opens, freeing you to be sensitive, vital, and creative.

Zen began with Buddha who sat outside meditating under a tree until one day he saw the morning star and was awakened. He exclaimed, "I, and the great earth and beings, simultaneously achieve the Way." He saw his essential nature which is the essential nature of the great earth and all beings. He saw that they are one interconnected whole. In the direct experience of wholeness you are healed and simultaneously you gain the vision to heal and preserve the great earth and all beings.

# BEING YOURSELF:

## *Living Your Life Fully*

To know and accept who you are and to really be yourself is healing. Feeling forced to present a false self or to keep up a false image chokes off your vitality and keeps you from being who you truly are. You are unique and no one else can be you. You are the expert on your life. You are the only one who can experience being you and who can live your life fully. You are the one who must decide for yourself to be healed and to be a healing presence in the world.

Recently, Alison, one of the women I teach nursing with, was in the hospital because she went into premature labor at twenty-eight weeks. She was on bedrest and sick as a dog from the medication she was given to stop the premature labor. The bright spot in this situation was that the nurse assigned to take care of her was Heather.

Heather was a student of Alison's several years earlier. Heather came from a small town in West Virginia. She was the first person in her family ever to go to college. She had to study really hard to make it through nursing school. She put her whole self into her nursing studies. She did all the reading assignments, she sat up in class and paid close attention, and she asked lots of good questions. During clinical studies she chose the most difficult patients to care for so she could learn as much as possible. And she didn't make drudgery out of it. She worked hard and she played hard. She made good friends among her classmates and went to the beach on breaks. In fact, one time I had to let her out of class early to go to court over a speeding ticket she had gotten on the way to the beach. Whatever she did she put her whole self into it. Heather is full of herself, but not selfish. In fact, she is exceptionally caring and compassionate. Her vitality and liveliness make her truly a healing presence.

So Alison was mighty glad to see Heather walk into the room to take care of her. True to form, Heather put her whole self into being Alison's nurse. She did thorough assessments, bathed her, helped her get into a comfortable position, brought a fan into the room to cool her off from the flushing effect of the medication, and brought her glasses of ginger ale. She helped her through some really tough days. Happily, eleven weeks later Alison gave birth to a healthy full-term baby.

The point of Zen is to really be yourself and to live your life fully. Sitting in the silence of meditation you notice what sensations arise in the body, what thoughts arise in the mind, and what feelings accompany the sensations and thoughts. Taking time to slow down and pay attention, you get to know yourself better and in subtler and subtler ways. Zen practice encourages you to see things just as they are and to see yourself just as you are. It encourages you to accept yourself just as you are. In this climate of self-acceptance and openness, new behaviors can emerge.

Self-acceptance is easier said than done. For example, can you accept your own body just as it is? Not how it will be when you lose ten pounds. Not how it will be when you exercise more regularly and become more fit and flexible. Can you accept it just as it is right now? Working as a nurse, you quickly learn that if you need to know how much a person weighs, you stand the person on the scale. You don't ask. A woman five feet four inches tall will stand there and tell you she weighs 130 pounds when really she weighs 150. It's difficult to accept yourself just as you are. This can be especially true when you are sick, weak, difficult to be with, or unable to give, at least the way you're used to. Although self-acceptance can be difficult, it is an essential step in the healing process.

Zen practice not only involves accepting yourself totally, including your strengths and limitations, but also learning to respect and honor yourself. You grow to appreciate the unique human being that you are. This opens you to live your life more fully and completely. When you meditate you put your whole self into sitting and are aware with every cell in your body. Putting the whole self into meditation teaches you how to put your whole self into each thing you do during the day.

At the same time the self is appreciated, developed, expressed, and lived out more fully, insight is gained into no-self. The insight gained through Zen practice is the direct experience that there is no separate self. This is called the experience of no-self, no-mind, emptiness, or nonduality. It is the simultaneous experience of a well-developed sense of self along with the experience of no-self that makes Zen such a powerful and transformative practice.

No-self does not mean a mousy sort of selflessness. Nor does it mean some kind of self-defeating martyrdom. It is the direct experience that there is no static thing that is the self. It is the direct experience that there is no separation between yourself and the rest of the universe. It is the direct experience of your essential nature that is one with the essential nature of the universe.

There is a Zen koan about self and no-self. Once Zen Master Rahulata said to his student Sanghanandi:

> *Since I am without a self,*
> *You should see the Self.*
> *Because if you make me your master,*
> *You will understand that the self is not the Self.*

When Sanghanandi heard this, his mind opened. The experience that there is no separate self, the experience of no-self, is not a grim sort of nothingness. It is vast as the universe and liberating.

In the verse to this koan it says, "How many times has the Self appeared with a different face!" My original face is each face I see. Seeing this, you would like the needs of each face, of each person, to be met. I have washed a lot of faces, the blood-streaked faces of newborn babies, the hot sweaty faces of children with fevers, the faces of people too sick to wash their own faces, and the face I see in the mirror each morning and evening. Each face I wash is my own original face.

For Christians the great commandment is, "You must love the Lord your God with all your heart, with all your soul, with all your strength, and with all your mind, and your neighbor as yourself." Usually we interpret this to mean that we should treat our neighbor the way we would like to be treated. Zen can help you deepen your experience of this teaching. Zen insight enables you to directly experience that your neighbor is yourself. There is no separation. This great commandment is very much in keeping with the Zen spirit of putting your whole self into each thing you do and seeing each person and everything in the universe as yourself. This is what is meant by no-self, that there is no separate self. When you experience yourself as not separate, you no longer feel fragmented, alienated, lost, or isolated. You experience your wholeness which is a healing experience.

There is a Zen koan about the expanded experience of self in which everything in the universe is experienced as the self. Zen Master Tan-hsia tested his student, Wu-kung, by asking him, "What is the self prior to the empty eon?" As soon as Wu-kung started to speak, Tan-hsia stopped him, saying, "You're noisy; go away for awhile." So Wu-kung went away and one day decided to take a hike up Po-yu Peak. As he climbed up the last stretch to the top of the mountain, he was suddenly awakened.

What did Wu-kung see up on Po-yu Peak that caused him to awaken? He saw trees, mountains, and fields extending in all directions. He saw deer, rabbits, birds, and bugs. He saw a stream winding down through the valley. He saw himself. Perhaps he stretched out his arms and said, "I am whole. I am alive!"

# DISCIPLINE:

## *You're Stronger Than You Think*

Often healing requires discipline. Sometimes it's the discipline required to exercise regularly or to stick to a particular diet. Sometimes you need to take medicine on a set schedule or change a dressing each day. Some people need to get more rest and relaxation on a regular basis. These things are not difficult to do, but we all know how much discipline it takes to follow through day after day and do what needs to be done to promote healing.

Sometimes healing takes great emotional strength to deal with unexpected setbacks without becoming so discouraged that you give up. One young man I took care of had been coping since childhood with diabetes, checking his blood sugar, being careful about the food he ate, and giving himself insulin injections every day. Despite his vigilant efforts he experienced several episodes of retinal hemorrhage. He sought out the best ophthalmologist he could find, got treatment for his eyes, and continued working with his endocrinologist to fine-tune his daily program of diabetes management. Shortly thereafter he had a heart attack requiring bypass surgery. Although he was deeply discouraged, he sought help from his doctors, nurses, family, friends, and coworkers, determined to get better, get back to work, and be there for his two school-age children. With discipline and determination he was able to get back on his feet and experience healing again and again.

Zen practice requires discipline and discipline builds strength. I remember when I first saw people doing Zen meditation, and considered doing it myself, the thought of sitting without leaning against anything was daunting. I didn't know if I could do it. I found, as many have found, that over time, with the correct cushion, bench, or front of a chair, it is not a great problem. It's a matter of finding the right balance. Gradually I built up to sitting comfortably for a twenty-five-minute period of meditation. It feels good to sit up straight and tall like a tree in the forest. Now I feel discomfort with slouching.

In addition to the posture, discipline is required to sit still and be silent. Silence and stillness are quite foreign in our noisy, complex, fast-paced culture. Often when I am getting ready to leave town and head for a Zen retreat, my mother will say, "I don't know why anyone would want to spend the whole weekend sitting on a little black cushion not talking to anyone." Although it is difficult for some people, others find it a pleasant respite or even an antidote to the business of life in the world today.

Once a friend, Glen, spoke movingly at his father's memorial service about his father's strength. His father had the ability to do hours of hard physical labor, chopping cords of wood, building, and repairing, well into his sixties and seventies. Glen told how he remembered working with his father repairing their cabin in the Adirondack Mountains when Glen was in his thirties and his dad was in his sixties. All day they crawled in and out from under the cabin fixing the plumbing. His dad worked long and hard yet he didn't seem to have the sore muscles that Glen had the next day. What impressed me most was that Glen said he learned that working hard like that increased his ability to work hard. In this sense you can say that strength begets strength.

Roshi Richardson often encouraged us onward during long days of sitting at intensive weeklong Zen retreats by saying, "Sit strongly." And of course she, in her seventies, sat strongly hour after hour, setting the pace for us youngsters. Mary Byrnes, who is also about the same age, with serious arthritis, could be seen sitting straight and still round after round, hour after hour. Because of the arthritis in her feet, she walked slowly by herself during walking meditation and then rejoined the group at the beginning of each sitting period. We knew that all this was being done during her week of vacation from her job as the administrator at a retirement home. She always said her job was taking care of the old folks. With elders like these to inspire us and set an example, we learn that we are stronger than we think we are.

There is a koan about strength that asks, "Why is it that a man of great strength does not lift up his legs?" This koan, like all the koans, is trying to shift your perception from your ordinary way of thinking and seeing things to experiencing the essential nature of phenomena. It is trying to move you, get you to lift your leg, and take another step. It is nudging you to take a leap from ordinary strength into the realm of unbounded strength and potential. Sitting in meditation you get in touch with your own inner strength and resources. When you experience that you are not separate from others and from the universe, you can draw on these unlimited resources to find the strength you need to keep going in difficult times.

The elegance and power of Zen is the combination of discipline and beauty integrated in the practice. The straight, disciplined sitting and walking goes on amid the beauty of an uncluttered hall, a flower, a bell, an open window, a gentle breeze, a bird calling out, and the graceful presence of others sitting in silence. The discipline creates the space and time to appreciate the astounding and subtle beauty of life.

The elegance and power of my work as a nurse also results from the integration of discipline and beauty. Nursing requires a tremendous amount of discipline— it's needed in order to assimilate large amounts of rapidly changing information, to use new technology, to complete tasks in a timely manner, to closely observe the moment-to-moment changes in the condition of seriously ill patients, and to be prepared for emergencies. Each shift the emergency cart is checked and the team is ready to spring into action with military precision the moment a person's heart stops beating.

Yet amid all this discipline the nurse maintains her humanity and relates to the human beings she is caring for. This is the beauty of nursing, the comforting touch, the clean sheets, the listening heart, the tears and the laughter, the shared experience. Both discipline and beauty are needed to heal and be whole.

In Zen practice, the physical discipline of sitting still, the mental discipline of choosing to remain in the present moment, and the emotional discipline of not denying what is right in front of you, combined with the beauty of deep silence, peace, and unity help you get in touch with your strength. Discipline builds the strength you need to heal yourself and others.

# SIMPLICITY:
## *"'Tis a Gift to Be Simple"*

There is a well-known Shaker song, "'Tis a gift to be simple, 'tis a gift to be free ..." Simplicity is healing. Simplicity frees you from worries, concerns, and distractions that keep you from joining in the dance and enjoying the beauty of the life that surrounds you each day. Are you free to experience each sunrise and greet each new day? Are you free to experience each sunset, letting go into a night of restful sleep? Each season, each change in the weather, comes to you simply asking to be experienced just as it is.

Often we are too busy or distracted to experience this. Sometimes it takes a serious, life-threatening illness to wake us up to what is essential and to the simple pleasures of life. One patient I took care of while he was recovering from an automobile accident said that it was the simplest things that brought him the greatest comfort and satisfaction. Getting off the respirator and being able to breathe on his own again was exhilarating. Standing in the shower with warm water running down over him felt so cleansing and soothing. Clean sheets and pajamas were so refreshing. A drink of water and a slice of toast were so satisfying. Walking the length of the hall felt like a tremendous accomplishment. A simple back rub was so comforting. He was deeply grateful for his family and simply to be alive.

As a nurse, I find that the simple things are as necessary to healing as complex medical treatments. Along with the use of sophisticated medical technology to cure disease, it is essential to meet basic human needs. It is essential to care for the human being amid the maze of equipment, tubes, and wires. Simple human presence, caring, and touch, provide needed balance in the high-tech hospital environment of today.

Simplicity is an antidote to the complexity of modern life. One can get buried under the mountains of paperwork required for everyday living. At the office often it takes over an hour just to answer phone messages, sort through the mail, and check the e-mail before beginning the day. At work in the hospital, often there is new equipment to be mastered before the day's work can be accomplished. New drugs come out almost daily. Lots of time is spent attending committee meetings, arguing with insurance companies, documenting, and evaluating. It seems that there is little time left to simply care for the patient. There is a great need to take the reins and simplify.

Simplicity is an aspect of Zen that I have always found particularly attractive. Zen is clear and uncluttered. There is an abundance of silence and few words. There is an aesthetic appreciation of simplicity that is expressed in the arrangement of a single flower or the careful preparation of a cup of tea. Zen practice is simple. It is simply sitting, breathing, walking, and living.

A friend, Leslie, decided to use the simplicity of Zen as a model for simplifying her life. She started by clearing the clutter from her office and her home. She got an extra filing cabinet for her office and was able to file or throw away the stacks of paper that had been piled high on her desk and bookcases for the past several years. She then had room for a small graceful plant on the top of her bookcase. At home she cleaned out her closets and cabinets and took three carloads of old clothes and odds and ends that she hadn't used in many years to the Salvation Army. Leslie found that her home and office felt so much brighter and more spacious. She said it was like lifting a weight off her shoulders. She felt less pressured and stressed and she felt like she had room to breathe.

The simplicity of Zen is its magnificence. Zen practice is one way to make some time and space for simply being alive—for simply living. Sitting in meditation morning and evening frees the mind of unnecessary clutter. You free the body to simply sit up tall and breathe. You place no layer of meaning or interpretation onto the simple experience of being alive. You simply sleep, wake up, take a shower, eat, drive, work, and play. Simplicity restores the balance and elegance of life.

Simplicity creates the time, space, and openness to experience the profound. A monk once asked Zen Master Tozan, "What is Buddha?" Tozan answered, "Three pounds of flax." When the monk asked, "What is Buddha?" he meant, "What is the essence of Zen?" or "What is the essence of life?" This exchange probably took place during the time of year when the flax was being harvested or its fibers were being spun into linen thread.

Tozan responded with something near at hand. Flax was something that was part of the everyday life of the monk. The profound, essential nature of yourself and the universe is near at hand; it is experienced in each simple activity of daily living.

Actually, life is both simple and complex. We share many simple human needs and emotions. At the same time we are each different and highly complex. Our physical differences are minute compared to our psychological and spiritual differences. Add to this our interdependence with everything else in the universe, and the complexity of life is beyond comprehension or imagination. The direct experience of the simplicity of essential nature balances and enriches the diversity and complexity of life.

I once received a card from a friend and on it was a quote by Gandhi, "May I live simply that others may simply live." I saved the card and have it on the bulletin board above my desk where I can see it each day. Gandhi was a master of simplicity. For him simplicity and spirituality went hand in hand. He dressed, ate, and lived simply. Each day he spent time at his spinning wheel making thread to weave into cloth. He was a role model not only for India, but also for us today. I often think of Gandhi as I recycle. There is such a great need to package the products we consume more simply in order to cut down on waste. We need to eat, dress, and live more simply if our beautiful planet is to survive. Through the direct experience of essential nature we see that there are no others, that we are one. If human beings, all beings, and the great earth are to survive, we must learn the lessons of simplicity. And so I pray, "May I live simply, that we may simply live."

Often patients become confused and overwhelmed with the complexity of their medical regimens. Sometimes I am able to sit down with a patient and help him organize and simplify his medication routine. We sit down together and go over the medications that need to be taken on an empty stomach and those that need to be taken with food. Some of them can be taken at the same time thereby cutting down on the number of times a day pills need to be taken. We try to coordinate the times for taking pills with mealtimes and bedtime when possible. All in all we try to come up with the simplest possible schedule. The simplest schedule is most likely to be followed successfully. Living simply helps us to simply live.

One summer out in Boulder, Colorado, my husband Charles, a friend named Alvin, and I walked down the street to eat at a little barbecue pit called Daddy Bruce's. Parked beside the tiny white clapboard building was a pick-up truck and on the side of it was painted, "God loves you and Daddy Bruce does too." While we were waiting for our food to be prepared, we read newspaper clippings that were taped to the walls of the restaurant telling how Daddy Bruce took five thousand servings of barbecue down to inner-city Denver on Thanksgiving Day to feed those in need. In the article he said that he did it because that was the number of people Jesus fed when he multiplied the loaves and the fishes.

When we picked up our order, Alvin asked the young man at the counter if he could have a straw for his coke. The young man launched into a heartfelt speech saying, "This is a basic place. We have lots of good food, but nothing extra." Alvin had to drink directly from the can and not sip through a straw. He ate his huge pile of barbecued ribs with his hands and afterward licked his lips and fingers like a child. He simply and heartily ate. It was a great meal with nothing extra.

When you simplify your life you do not feel pulled in all directions and are free to enjoy the simple pleasures each day has to offer. Simplicity creates the time and space for you to experience healing. Simplicity frees you to help meet the basic needs of others so they too can experience healing.

# BEING ORDINARY:
## *The Ordinary Is Extraordinary*

Often we take for granted just being ordinary. We feel the constant pressure to compete, to excel, and to be special. The fact is most people are average with respect to any particular human characteristic. That is the definition of average. And yet many are not satisfied with average or ordinary and tend to be discontent and always striving. It is a great relief and healing when you realize that just being ordinary and your ordinary life are wonderful gifts.

When people are ill often they long to return to their ordinary life and to be able to do the things they ordinarily do like climbing a flight of stairs, going grocery shopping, or driving a car. Many times when I have taken care of young people with a serious illness like diabetes they've felt sad and frustrated because they had to stick to a special diet and take insulin while all the other kids could eat whatever they wanted and just got to be normal. They longed to be able to do the ordinary things in life like go to school, get a job, get married, and have a baby. Many worked very hard to accomplish these goals.

Zen practice helps you fully appreciate your ordinary life. With awareness, the ordinary becomes extraordinary. You need to pay attention to what you are doing. Be one with each task, action, or thing. In this way you will discover your true nature and the true nature of each thing will shine through, illuminating everyday life. You will perceive the richness of life and feel blessed just to be an ordinary person.

When vacuuming pay attention to moving the vacuum cleaner over each area of the carpet without thinking about what you will do next or what you would rather be doing. When driving attend to the road in front of you, the traffic, and your hold on the steering wheel. Don't be daydreaming with your mind somewhere else and arrive not knowing how you got there. When doing paperwork, attend to writing checks, typing memos, and filing receipts. Don't be fragmented, preoccupied, or separate from each activity of your life. When you are fully present and aware you wake up to the wonder of your ordinary mind.

Those of you who have children or are primary schoolteachers have seen the ordinary mind of a child. Children's minds are bright, sensitive, curious, and like a sponge. They are enthusiastic about pouring water, erasing the chalkboard, baking a cake, or shoveling sand. They like to put their hands and their whole selves into each thing they do. They give you a glimpse of your ordinary mind.

In Zen meditation you become fully awake and present to the wonder of your ordinary mind. One day Joshu asked Zen Master Nansen, "What is the Way?" Nansen answered, "The ordinary mind is the Way." Joshu asked, "Should I direct myself toward it or not?"

Nansen answered, "If you try to turn toward it, you go against it."

Nansen says that ordinary mind is the Way. Joshu wonders how he can find it or know it. In the sutra, "The Identity of the Relative and Absolute" it says, "If you do not see the Way, you do not see it even as you walk on it." You don't need to search elsewhere for it. It is right here now in your ordinary life.

Ordinary mind does not mean a mind caught up in habitual patterns of thinking, daydreaming, worrying, or clinging. It does not mean a mind bound up in concepts, theories, preconceived ideas, or fixed opinions. Ordinary mind is the mind that is fresh and open to limitless possibilities. It is the mind that is free to experience the circumstances and seasons of our life. This is beautifully conveyed in the Zen verse:

> *The spring flowers, the moon in autumn,*
> *The cool breezes of summer, the winter's snow:*
> *If idle concerns do not cloud the mind,*
> *This is the happiest season.*

Sitting silent and still in meditation allows the mind to settle and become clear. In this clarity you are able to see the nature of your mind. It is empty, vast, and bright. You see that it is one with everything. Your mind is nothing other than each ordinary thing it perceives. Each particular thing contains the whole. Ordinary mind is the mind that is not separate from the whole as it manifests in the ordinary people, events, and things in your everyday life.

The simultaneous experiencing of the universal and the particular brings new vitality and freshness to life. The water in the shower in the morning feels wetter and more refreshing. The sky looks bluer and the trees a thousand shades of green. The tea tastes warmer and the muffin sweeter. When you sit, sitting is the Way. When you drive, driving is the Way. When you swim, swimming is the Way. An ordinary life is a life well worth living.

There is a Zen koan that says, "If you meet a man on the path who has accomplished the Way, do not greet him with words or silence. Tell me, how will you greet him?" How would you know if a person you meet on the path is a person who has accomplished the Way? It is said that those who have truly accomplished the Way appear very ordinary. Yamada Roshi is a good example of this. Dressed in a business suit and hat, he rode the commuter train each day to work and back, blending in with the crowd. In the evenings and on weekends he worked with Zen students who came to Kamakura from all over the world to do Zen meditation and study with him. I have often ridden the PATH from Jersey City into Manhattan with Roshi Kennedy when he is going into his office to see psychotherapy clients. He looks like an ordinary American of Irish descent with his wool cap and St. Peter's College jacket, sitting on a dingy crowded subway train and then walking briskly down the busy sidewalk to work.

So the question becomes, how do you greet any human being? How do you greet each morning, each evening, each bite of food that you eat, each job that needs to be done? Are you alert to each aspect of your ordinary life?

One day at work at the psychiatric hospital there was a young man with bipolar disorder who was manic, hallucinating, and very labile. He was bothering the other patients with his nonstop commentary and from time to time he erupted into threats and violent gestures. A nurse offered to shampoo his hair for him, partly because he needed help getting cleaned up, and partly in an attempt to distract, soothe, and calm him. At first he enjoyed the attention and the warm water flowing over his head. But then, while the nurse gently massaged the shampoo into his hair, he began accusing her of being too rough and of digging her fingernails into his scalp. At one point a little soapy water ran down the side of his face. He reached up, rubbed it off, and held out his hand and said, "See, I'm bleeding." She said, "That's not blood. It's water." He shouted, "Then why is it as red as that chair over there?" He had been ill like this for several months and none of the medications were helping. He wished he had an ordinary mind.

When you realize and fully appreciate the incredible gift that an ordinary mind and an ordinary life are, you are healed of your dissatisfaction and discontent. Your endless seeking after more comes to an end and you feel complete and whole just as you are.

# EXPERIENCING DIRECTLY:
## *Knowing for Yourself*

Illness and healing are direct human experiences. Many people get coronary artery disease and the disease is largely the same for each of them. The arteries become blocked and adequate amounts of blood cannot flow to the heart. However the human experience of having coronary artery disease, the physical sensations, the emotions, the meaning of the illness to the individual, and the impact of the illness on the individual's life are unique for each person experiencing the disease. The process of healing is also unique for each person who must experience wholeness for him or herself as the circumstances of life unfold moment by moment.

Many nurses and physicians I have worked with have told me that even though they took care of many people with many types of illness, it wasn't until they experienced serious illness themselves that they gained a real understanding of what it is like to be seriously ill. They found that through their own direct experience of illness they gained an increased sensitivity in caring for others.

Many years ago I read the Russian novel *One Day in the Life of Ivan Denisovich*. I still remember how moved I was when Ivan, who was sick and freezing to death in a Siberian prison camp, went to work outdoors in subzero temperatures thinking to himself, "How can you expect a man who's warm to understand a man who's cold?" When I'm outdoors on a particularly cold January night I think of this passage and think to myself that only now can I feel a small portion of what it is like to be homeless in the wintertime.

Zen is also learned through experience. You don't just talk about Zen, you do it. You sit in meditation, then you do walking meditation, and then you sit again. When New River Zen Community offers introductory Zen workshops, we have to warn people that we will be talking and explaining only a small part of the day. It will not be a day of lecture and discussion. Most of the day will be spent actually doing it. Zen is a lived experience.

Many people have read books about Zen and think that they know all about it. Some are experts on the history of Zen, the philosophy of Zen, or the poetry of Zen. But knowing about Zen is not the same as knowing Zen itself. You can't really know what Zen is until you do it and experience it. Zen is not something that is known with the intellect or head alone. It involves the body, the whole person, and the whole universe. It must be directly experienced for yourself. Zen is life. You cannot learn about life from a textbook alone. You have to go out and live it for yourself.

To experience directly is to know and not know simultaneously. There is a well-known Zen story about a Zen student, Hakuin, who gave an intellectual answer to his teacher's question. His teacher responded by suddenly grabbing and twisting Hakuin's nose. Hakuin yelled out, "*ouch*." This was the genuine response that the teacher was leading the student toward. Direct experience is knowing for yourself how it feels. It is living right in this moment, even if this moment is "*ouch*." It is not being separated from the experience by thought about the experience or thought about the meaning of the experience. It is knowing intimately through direct experience. At the same time it is "not knowing" in the sense of not being stuck in the head and not trying to grasp and hold on to experiences intellectually.

Many people who have experienced being the primary caregiver for an ill family member in the home have told me that they don't feel people who have never been in that situation understand how limiting and totally exhausting it is. For several years, Martha, a woman in her early seventies, took care of her eighty-one-year-old husband after he had a stroke that left him incontinent and unable to walk, bathe, dress, or feed himself independently. Medicare only paid for an aide to come to the home and help with his care for three hours three times a week. Luckily a volunteer from a local senior citizen organization, who had cared for her own husband until his death two years before, came to the house to sit with Martha's husband for three hours each Thursday afternoon. It was Martha's only chance to get out of the house to go grocery shopping, to the post office, and to the bank. Perhaps if more people understood the experience of providing twenty-four-hour care for a dependent family member, more resources would be allocated to assist family caregivers so they don't become completely exhausted and isolated.

Direct experience can help us become more understanding of others and of ourselves. One day Zen Master Ananda asked his student Sanavasa, "What kind of thing is the original unborn nature of all things?" Sanavasa could not answer so Ananda pulled on the corner of Sanavasa's robe. With this gesture Sanavasa was awakened. Through this gesture Ananda was showing his student that the experience of the original unborn nature of all things is personal. It must be experienced directly by Sanavasa and by each of us. It is not a thing or an object. It is a personal experience. In the words of Zen Master Mumon, "You will know yourself and for yourself only."

There is a beautiful Zen verse about knowing for yourself and for yourself only:

> By acquiring the marrow, you will know the clarity
> of what you found;
> Lun-pien still possesses subtleties he does not pass on.

You can go deep and directly experience the essence of yourself, of life, and of the universe. The clarity of your experience makes you aware of infinite subtleties—each perceived moment to moment. So a glimpse of your essential nature is a beginning, not an end. It is knowing and at the same time opening yourself to not knowing. Such a glimpse cannot be communicated in words or given to others. Others must experience their essential nature for themselves.

The experience of your essential nature shows you that you should not be separated from life itself by thoughts about life. In the first koan many Zen students work on, a monk asks Zen Master Joshu if a dog has Buddha nature or not. Joshu answers "Mu!" The following is a verse about this exchange between Joshu and the monk:

*Dog! Buddha nature!*
*The perfect manifestation, the absolute command;*
*A little "has" or "has not,"*
*And body is lost! Life is lost!*

When you step back from life itself, into thought about life, you step back into your head and your body is lost. You become divided and preoccupied by dualistic thoughts such as "has" or "has not." Absorbed in division and preoccupied with theoretical speculation, you miss your precious life. Life itself slips by without being fully experienced, appreciated, and lived robustly.

As a nursing professor, some days I lecture to a large group of students in the classroom and some days I take eight or ten students with me to the hospital to take care of patients. I devote great effort and creativity in the classroom trying to convey to the students the human experience of having a serious life-threatening or chronic illness. But it isn't until they have the direct experience in the hospital of caring for real people with real problems that they make a connection and really learn. It isn't until they spend a day in the hospital face-to-face, caring for a young person their own age who has AIDS, that they begin to directly experience this reality. With the direct experience of being with and caring for a real person who has AIDS, the lights go on. Often the students are deeply moved and it is this human-to-human experience, rather than the many lectures that they have heard on the topic, that leads them to reconsider the safety of their own behaviors. Direct experience results in learning that stays with the students and forms them into competent and caring nurses. The experience of learning to heal others can have a healing effect on your own behavior and life.

Many times you must rely on direct experience to determine what is helping you heal and what does not seem to be working. Doctors and nurses need your input about how you are feeling and whether or not your symptoms are improving. Working in partnership with your health care provider, having an open mind, and being willing to try reasonable treatments and lifestyle changes often lead to finding a course of action that is healing for you. Only you can experience your own healing.

# PAYING ATTENTION:
## *Staying Awake and Alert*

Paying attention is the moment-to-moment choice to see, hear, smell, taste, and feel many of the things we have come to take for granted and therefore often overlook or ignore. Really paying attention is an active process that requires your whole body, mind, and spirit and unites your whole body, mind, and spirit. Attention wakes you up and connects you with the people, things, and events you attend to. To heal yourself you need to pay attention moment by moment to your life as it unfolds before your very eyes.

Paying attention is also necessary to recognize danger and prevent illness and accidents. Anyone caring for toddlers knows the constant attention that is needed to keep them safe. The cleaning supplies and medicines need to be locked out of reach, the stairways gated, and the electric outlets covered. If you have a family history of heart disease, you need to pay attention to your diet, exercise, alcohol consumption, cholesterol, and stress level. When you are driving you need to be alert and constantly pay attention in order to prevent accidents. As a nurse I have to pay attention to the details of where the nerves, blood vessels, bones, and muscles are located in order to give an injection safely. Paying attention is essential to promoting health and preventing disease and injury.

When you pay attention to others, they can feel their value and worth as human beings. In order to really pay attention to another, you need to stop being absorbed in your own mental dialogue and really listen to what the other person is saying and trying to express. This involves letting go of your own opinions and point of view long enough to hear the other's experience, perspective, feelings, and needs. Paying attention is an active process of being with, listening, and responding moment to moment.

My first job as a nurse was working night shift in a neonatal intensive care unit. The typical night was spent alternately sitting or standing at the bedside of a single, critically ill two-pound premature infant providing warmth, fluids, and oxygen. All night was spent watching the tiny chest rising and falling; observing the color—pink, mottled, or pale; protecting the thin fragile skin, skin so thin you could see through it; positioning the baby in a cradle of sheepskin and rolled-up cloth diapers; attending to and caring for a human infant amid a maze of machinery and tubing; staying awake all night paying attention.

With this kind of attention, you are really able to see what is right in front of you, just as it is, moment by moment, and respond accordingly. In really seeing this unique and particular infant, you are united with all infants struggling to live and with all women around the world and down the ages who have cared for sick babies. The cry of this tiny infant is heard throughout the universe.

When a baby could breathe without the help of a respirator, he or she was placed in an isolette. Simultaneously caring for several babies in isolettes, it was always someone's turn to be wrapped in a blanket, held, rocked, and either tube or bottle-fed. All the while, my ear was kept tuned to the chorus of monitors rhythmically beeping out each baby's heartbeat. If a heartbeat slowed it meant a baby had forgotten to breathe momentarily and he or she promptly received a rub on the back. "Come on, wake up and breathe." With this gentle reminder, the baby started to breathe again and the heartbeat came back up to speed. With constant attention most of the babies did well and came back a year or two later as lively toddlers to say hello and thank you.

Zen practice is paying attention moment to moment, whatever your circumstances. In paying attention to and fully experiencing both the joy and pain of life, your life is whole and rich, and you are healed.

When beginning Zen practice, you are often instructed to sit up and pay attention to your breath. Later on your practice may become "just sitting," which means paying attention to just sitting in the present moment, right here and now. In both of these practices, when you notice you have drifted off into thinking, or planning, or remembering, or daydreaming, you bring your attention back to your breath or to just sitting right here and now. Paying attention is an active choice to return to your breath or sitting.

During Zen meditation there is no need to strain to clear your mind of thoughts. Thoughts will drift through your mind like clouds through the sky. Rather than intentionally continuing the line of thought, you choose to come back to paying attention to the breath or to just sitting in the present moment. You simply sit with awareness in the present moment and let go of your habitual thoughts and preoccupations. Paying attention is healing. It frees your mind and energy to live vitally each vibrant moment.

Recently while teaching a nursing class, I became concerned because one of the student nurses fell asleep in class on several occasions. At first I was worried that the class was boring, but when I spoke with her she assured me that was not the problem. She said she was falling asleep because she had been staying up too late studying for critical care quizzes. The next day she told me she fell asleep in her critical care class that morning. Her critical care professor tapped her on the shoulder and said, "Wake up or go home." That's exactly what the head monk in the Zen hall would say. If you are not awake and paying attention, you will not learn, see, or hear and it sets up a lethargic atmosphere for others. There is a palpable energy in the room when a group sits in meditation together and each person is wakeful and attentive.

A friend whose husband has cancer shared with me that she and her husband are taking the time now to pay attention to every season. On fall days they go out for walks across the fields and through the woods and really pay attention to the sunlight dancing on the gold, orange, and red leaves. On snowy winter days they build a fire in the fireplace and listen to the crackle and snap and feel the warmth on their skin. These times are healing for them as individuals and as a couple and they feel they are drinking in all of life that they can while they have the chance.

Zen Master Zuigan worked very hard every day to wake up and pay attention. Each day he called out to himself, "Master!" He answered himself, "Yes!" Then he called out to himself again, "Thoroughly awake! Thoroughly awake!" He answered, "Yes! Yes!"

Every day when you sit down to meditate, it is a way to call out to yourself, "Are you awake? Are you paying attention?" Even if you can't be awake and attentive all the time, you can set aside a meditation period of twenty-five minutes to be thoroughly awake and paying attention. With practice this will carry over into being wakeful and attentive more and more of each day. When you are thoroughly awake and attentive you are not separate from life. You are whole and fully alive.

# OPENING:

## *Having an Open Mind and Heart*

When you are open-minded, you do not hold onto fixed views or opinions. Holding on to a particular view, theory, or opinion can create blinders that prevent you from seeing things as they are. Your views, theories, and opinions can block you from seeing something new.

Being open-minded means being nonjudgmental. This involves letting go of the habit of constantly evaluating things in terms of good or bad, like or dislike, agree or disagree. Not judging allows you to see things just as they are. Much suffering is generated by expectations of how life should be or of how you should be. Not judging frees you from your shoulds and your endless expectations. When you are open you are free to be who you are and to embrace the world as it is. This open embrace of yourself and others creates a climate of healing.

As a nurse I find I need to be open and nonjudgmental. I need to be open and fully present to patients' feelings and experiences, not distracted by mentally planning a reply or generating a solution. When I am open to the patient, the patient is free to speak and question openly and to hear the answer that lies in his or her own heart. When I am open, I can enter into a human-to-human relationship that is healing for both the patient and me.

Once I took care of a newborn infant who went

through drug withdrawal during the first days of his life. His mother was an unmarried teenager who was addicted to drugs. We kept the baby in a quiet corner of the nursery with a receiving blanket draped over the isolette to cut down on stimulation and prevent seizures. Seeing her baby's shakiness, hearing his high-pitched cry, and watching us administer tapering doses of phenobarbital, his mother was remorseful for what she had done. Rather than rejecting her, I listened and interacted with her openly and tried to build on her strengths, resources, and love for her baby. In an atmosphere of openness and acceptance, she was able to admit the extent of her drug problem and seek treatment. She joined Narcotics Anonymous and said that the openness, honesty, and support of the people in the group were helping her stay off of drugs and blossom into the mother she wanted to be.

Zen practice is being open. It is the process of opening to your essential nature and the essential nature of the universe. It is being present and open to each particular thing just as it is. It is having an open mind and expanded vision so that you blossom like a flower in the sun.

One day Zen Master Gen gestured for two monks to roll up the blinds. The two monks rolled up the blinds in exactly the same way. Gen said, "One has gained, one has lost." Gen could sense this in the posture, movements, subtle gestures, and facial expression of the two monks. One monk was completely open and free. The other monk was still holding on to his conditioned way of being.

With every loss, there is a gain. When we roll up the

blinds of our minds we lose our old habits of thought and our old views. At the same time we open to something new and gain insight and expanded vision. There is a Zen verse that describes this expanded vision:

> *Rolling up the blinds, the great sky is open,*
> *But the great sky does not come up to Zen.*

In rolling up the blinds, you let go and open to your essential nature that is empty and vast like the sky. But Zen practice doesn't let you stop there and get stuck in emptiness. You must let go of trying to hold on to emptiness and open to the majesty of emptiness as it manifests in people, animals, plants, earth, stars, and galaxies. Looking through the window with the blinds rolled up, the view is spectacular and always changing.

Often taking care of patients in the hospital, I help them get up and showered or bathed in the morning and after placing their breakfast on their over-bed table, I open the blinds and let the new day shine in. Most of the rooms have a view looking out over the city. You can see the mountains in the background. Opening the blinds and connecting with the world going on outside the hospital has a healing effect on both me and on the patient. It makes our day richer, more colorful, and fuller.

Bluegrass and gospel music are very popular down here in the Appalachian Mountains where I live. One song contains the line, "I have opened up to heaven all the windows of my soul." Complete opening is a physical, psychological, and spiritual process. Physically you open by releasing the tension you are holding in your body. Also, you can physically open the blinds and windows of the room you are in. At some Zen centers the windows in the Zen hall are kept open even in the winter to keep the meditators fresh and awake. At times a gale wind blows through the room. One time I even ended up with snowflakes on my shoulders by the end of the meditation period. Psychologically you open your mind and heart. You let go of your conditioned ways of thinking, let down your defenses, and let go of your boundaries. You need the flexibility to be able to let down the walls you have constructed around yourself and become open, vulnerable, sensitive, and alive. Spiritually, you open yourself to nonseparation, and in doing so, experience wholeness and intimacy.

One day in early May I was doing some spring-cleaning and decided to wash the windows. After washing the windows both inside and out, I could see so much more clearly and the colors were more vibrant. Then I opened all the windows and there was no separation at all between inside and outside. A cool refreshing breeze blew through the house carrying with it the fragrance of blossoms, grass, and earth, and the songs of birds, children, and lawnmowers. It woke up my senses and I felt one with the season.

When you sit in Zen meditation your shoulders are back so your chest opens. Your spine is erect and your pelvis tilted slightly forward so your abdomen is open. Your head does not fall forward so your throat is open.

This posture allows full, natural, open breathing. During Zen meditation your eyes are open so you don't drift off into dreamland. Sitting alert with your eyes open you are always ready for a further insight, awakening, or opening. Also your hands are open. Open hands are hands that are not grasping. A hand that is clinging and grasping is a tight fist. In letting go your hand opens. Your open hands are relaxed and receptive, ready to receive something new.

One of my favorite poems is Walt Whitman's "Song of the Open Road." He sings:

> *Afoot and light-hearted I take to the open road,*
> *Healthy, free, the world before me,*
> *The long brown path before me leading wherever*
> *    I choose.*

If we are open, we are healthy and free. We are free to choose from the thousands of paths that open before us. The road of life is not always easy, but it is open to us, offering limitless possibilities.

# PERSEVERANCE:
## Keep on Going

Experiencing wholeness is not an end state. Although we are each already whole, being aware of our wholeness is an ongoing moment-by-moment process. Living your life in light of your wholeness is also a moment-by-moment endeavor. It is not something that is accomplished once and for all, but rather is an ongoing process of acting in accord with what you are seeing right now.

Healing is also an ongoing process. Rather than saying you are healed, you can say you are healing. People who are experiencing the process of healing are best able to help others heal. When in the process of healing you are vulnerable, sensitive, and open to transformation. Manifesting these qualities allows others to resonate with these qualities and open to the healing process. When a healer and a person in need of healing come together, both participate in the healing process and both learn, change, and grow through the interaction.

One woman I took care of named Sara had multiple sclerosis. She took excellent care of herself and received first class medical care at a clinic that specialized in treating diseases like multiple sclerosis. At times she experienced remissions of her illness and then it would get worse again. Sara got very discouraged with each recurrence. During these times she found that it was best for her to acknowledge her feelings of sadness, anger, and discouragement and take time to feel them. Then she was ready to let those feelings move to the periphery as she turned her attention to living each day to the fullest, one day at a time. Meditation was one of her self-care strategies. She said it helped her get in touch with her feelings and at the same time remain open to the rest of what each day had to offer her. It helped her keep on going. Working with Sara helped me learn how to keep on going, living life fully despite the setbacks or disappointments encountered along the way.

One of my favorite koans asks, "How do you go straight up a narrow mountain path with forty-nine curves?" This koan has much to teach us about perseverance. It reminds me of the time I hiked to the bottom of the Grand Canyon and was barely able to get myself up out of the canyon again. I put one foot in front of the other following switchback after switchback up the nearly vertical canyon wall. Along the sides of the trail lay sleeping bags, backpacks, jackets, and extra food left behind by previous hikers trying to lighten their loads in an effort to make it up to the rim. I walked slowly upward hour after hour with frequent breaks to sit on a rock and rest. When I finally made it to the rim, I went straight to Bright Angel Lodge and ate a large fruit salad. I thought I had reached heaven until I finished eating and tried to get up from the table to walk.

Going straight up a narrow mountain path with forty-nine curves means that we keep going despite difficulties or obstacles. It also suggests that we be willing to change direction when needed. We need to be persistent without clinging to fixed views, beliefs, or opinions. We are persistent yet flexible, teachable, and willing to learn. At times we may need to stop and rest and get our bearings. As we proceed up the path we are willing to immediately alter our course as soon as we see we are headed in the wrong direction. Each step on the path is all there is and yet we keep going.

When I think of perseverance, a little premie I took care of named Courtney comes to mind. She was in the neonatal intensive care unit for over four months. For several years after that she and her mom stopped by from time to time to visit and show off her latest accomplishments. At two years old she was just learning to walk. She finally got so she could walk with a walker and then she worked hard every day with her physical therapist, parents, and teachers to learn to walk without her walker. Her perseverance in trying over and over again and her steady progress were an inspiration to keep going.

Learning a new skill requires perseverance. If you want to learn to play the piano, you have to make time to practice each day. It takes persistence to master the basics, but with regular practice you progress to the enjoyment of playing a beautiful song or to the creativity of composing new music. Zen meditation also requires perseverance in making time to practice each day and as with playing the piano, a good teacher can be a great help. With regular meditation practice you will master the basics. As you continue meditating, insights will naturally occur and you will grow in your awareness of the wholeness of life.

In your awareness of wholeness and in your actualization in daily life of what you see, Zen encourages you to keep going. Sometimes you may be content to stay where you are or tempted to leave well enough alone. But Zen urges you onward, never taking a backward step. There is a koan that asks, "How will you step forward from the top of a hundred-foot pole?" An eminent Zen master once commented on this koan saying, "Even though one who is sitting on the top of a hundred-foot pole has entered realization, it is not yet real. He must step forward from the top of the pole and manifest his whole body throughout the world in the ten directions."

The hundred-foot pole represents the vertical or the ascending process. Through the deep silence of meditation, you experience essential nature, nonduality, or emptiness. This is a vast and liberating experience, but it is not the end point. It is just the beginning. You must step forward from the top of the hundred-foot pole to manifest this broad vision and freedom in daily life. Stepping forward to live life with freedom and compassion is the horizontal or descending process. You keep meditating and stepping forth, never getting stuck in any position or static state.

We encounter this theme in scripture also. "Foxes have holes and the birds of the air have nests, but the Son of Man has nowhere to lay his head." There is no resting place where you can complacently remain. Realization and the actualization of the love and freedom that you experience require ongoing effort day by day. It is not a once and for all matter. You are called to keep going.

We keep going because there is infinite subtlety to be perceived and profound healing to be experienced. Even though we ascend to the top of the hundred-foot pole and experience wholeness, we do not stop there. Wholeness manifests in an infinite number of forms—each changing from moment to moment. Wholeness and healing are not grasped and held on to once and for all. They are experienced moment by moment, as we step forward into life, one step after the next with each step completely new and infinitely subtle. So persevere and keep on going!

II

VITAL SIGNS:
CHANGES THAT COME
THROUGH HEALING

# NOT KNOWING:

*Journey into the Unknown*

There is much that cannot be known by thinking or reasoning. There are other ways of knowing and there are mysteries that cannot be grasped intellectually. Healing often comes through opening to other ways of knowing, to the mystery of life, and to not knowing. In opening to both knowing and not knowing, you come face to face with the wonder of life and to its boundless possibilities.

When we are studying difficult subjects like chemistry, physiology, mathematics, or philosophy, and we finally comprehend some principle or process, we say, "Oh, now I get it. Now I grasp the idea." This kind of thinking and knowing is very useful, but it is not enough. We must also be able to release our grip, stop our mental grasping, and open to something larger. This is what we call not knowing. We need the mental flexibility to both know and not know.

Not knowing is important in interpersonal relationships. There is respect and reverence in communicating to other people that you don't know them, their life experiences, and their feelings. When some great loss occurs, you don't say, "I know how you feel." You don't know. All you can say is, "I'm so sorry." In not knowing, you honor their unique experience, their unique expression, and their unique truth. Rather than assuming that you already know them, you are more attentive and open to learn more about them. It is a vital, sensitive, dynamic way of relating.

Charles and I have been married for over thirty years. You may think that after all these years I know Charles. I do know what he likes to eat. Often in a restaurant he looks at the menu and asks me, "What would I like?" I know what size and color shirt he likes and what music he prefers. But there are many things about Charles I do not know. He continues to surprise me. In fact, he amazes me. As the Zen saying goes, "Not knowing is most intimate."

Zen has no dogma, no doctrine, and no creed. Rather than delineating what we know or believe, the emphasis is on opening to what we don't know. We acknowledge and are present to the vast unknown. There is a beautiful Zen verse that communicates the essence of not knowing:

> *Moonlight reflected in the bottom of the pond*
> *is bright in the sky:*
> *The water reaching to the sky is totally clear and pure.*
> *Though you scoop it up repeatedly and try to know it,*
> *Vast, clarifying all, it remains unknown.*

Not knowing is a way of seeing that clarifies your vision, although it can't be grasped or held on to. Perceiving in this way, you see that there is nothing that can be grasped or held on to. Not knowing frees you to appreciate and serve vast beauty and mystery.

A man once came to see me in an individual meeting at a Zen retreat and said, "When I sit in meditation, I have in my mind the idea of unity. Is that what I should be doing?" I replied, "No. No idea, no matter how profound, should be created or held on to. Any concept you create limits your perception of reality, which is boundless. In not knowing, you are open to limitless possibilities."

Not knowing does not mean ignorance. It means not being a know-it-all. Nobody likes a know-it-all. They are boorish and hard to bear. They are lacking in humility.

Maezumi Roshi and Glassman Roshi titled one of their books *The Hazy Moon of Enlightenment*. This title emphasizes that enlightenment is a journey into the unknown. It is not static and known. It is a deep appreciation of the great mystery. It is an experience of infinite subtlety that cannot be fully communicated. Roshi Kennedy has often emphasized that we can say nothing about the great mystery. We don't give it a name. It is beyond thoughts, words, and images.

Living here in the Blue Ridge Mountains, sometimes the vista is clear as far as the eye can see, and sometimes it's shrouded in mist. The hazy fog and mist enhance the beauty of the mountains and give them their blue color, rolling off into the distance, ridge after ridge. Our path in life is sometimes clear and sometimes shrouded in mist. We don't know what lies just beyond the next ridge. Rather than being disturbed by this we can accept it as part of the mystery and spontaneity of life. There can be a sense of excitement in not knowing the whole story every step of the way.

In the Book of Job there is a magnificent passage about not knowing. Yahweh challenges Job with a series of questions such as, "Who pent up the sea behind closed

doors when it leaped tumultuous out of the womb?"
"Who begets the dewdrops?" "Do you know how mountain goats give birth, or have you ever watched the hinds
in labor?" In the end, Job concedes saying, "I have been
holding forth on matters I cannot understand, on marvels
beyond me and my knowledge."

What do we do when we do not know and yet must
deal with matters beyond our knowledge and understanding? Once I took care of a nine-year-old little girl
named Tara during the last three weeks of her life. She
had a wonderful team of brilliant and dedicated pediatric oncologists trying to cure her leukemia. They tried
everything the best medical researchers knew to do.
What do we do when we do not know? Tara had severe
diarrhea and her mouth was all bloody and crusted. I was
one of her nurses and we kept her as clean and comfortable as possible and gave her plenty of popsicles and pud-
ding and ice cream. We told stories, made scrapbooks,
played games, sang, and talked. Although Tara was a big
nine-year-old, she enjoyed being held in my arms and
rocked in the rocking chair like a baby. We did this during
the especially tough times so her mother would feel comfortable taking a break and going down to the cafeteria
for a warm meal. When we don't know what to do, all we
can do is be with, all we can do is love completely.

You live your life not knowing what comes next. You
need to make friends with not knowing. By going to the
heart of the matter you will know, you will be intimate,
and at the same time you will not know.

# EMPTINESS:

## *Vast and Boundless Like the Sky*

Emptying involves letting go of thoughts, worries, and barriers you have erected to protect yourself. Many people feel weighted down and overwhelmed by the demands and responsibilities of their lives. They feel cut off and isolated from the people around them. When you lighten the load and let down the walls you have built around yourself, there is a release, a great sense of freedom, increased sensitivity, and abundant vitality. Empty of boundaries you become aware of unity and wholeness.

Sometimes you have a head too full to hear another's point of view. Sometimes you have a schedule too full to even take a breath. Emptying is a way to create some time and space for yourself and others. Working in a time-pressured job like nursing, emptying is an essential survival skill. In order to really listen to and hear what patients are telling me about their experiences, I take a moment to take a breath, let go of the tension from my body, and stop generating thoughts about other things or the situation at hand. In this space, I receive and hear them. When we feel heard and understood, we connect as human beings. These moments are as healing as medicine and as nourishing as good food.

Zen is a process of emptying. You empty yourself of thoughts, words, categories, concepts, theories, images, and opinions. You empty yourself of expectations and accept life just as it is. You empty yourself of clinging, thereby releasing the muscle tension in the body resulting from holding, blocking, and guarding. Being empty of boundaries, you experience no separation.

At the beginning of a Zen retreat last summer, Roshi Kennedy said, "If you are blessed far beyond what you deserve, you will leave this retreat empty-handed." Emptiness is essential to the spirit of Zen. In the context of Zen, emptiness is not nihilism. It is not a void. It is not loneliness. It is not a black hole. The experience of emptiness is the experience of no boundaries and the experience that you are not separate. It is the experience of oneness. It is vast and boundless as the empty sky. It extends to the ends of the universe, unobstructed.

Zen Master Keizan once commented, "When emptiness is struck, it makes an echo, and thus all sounds are manifested. When emptiness is transformed, all things are manifested and, therefore, forms are distinguished. Do not think that emptiness is not forms, nor think that emptiness is not sounds." Keizan is helping us see that emptiness is not a thing or a state, emptiness is everything, just as it is. Emptiness is fullness.

There is a well-known Zen saying, "First there is a mountain, then there is no mountain, then there is." Most people's experience of reality is that there is a mountain. When we first experience emptiness, it is experienced as "there is no mountain." But many Zen masters have warned against getting stuck in emptiness. They immediately move you on from "no mountain" to "then there is." Having experienced emptiness, you can develop the capacity to experience emptiness and the mountain simultaneously. The mountain is emptiness. Emptiness is experienced in the form of a mountain. Emptiness manifests in forms such as mountains, trees, you, and me. All of this must be experienced for yourself. It can't be known on an intellectual level. Each person must engage in the process of emptying him or herself.

Zen Master Keizan tells us, "Even if you are thorough and meticulous, and by all means put an end to all things and make them utterly empty. There is still something that cannot be emptied." What is left when everything is emptied? What is it that cannot be emptied? If you engage in this process, you will experience directly what it is that cannot be emptied.

There is a Zen verse that says:

> *Seeking it oneself with empty hands,*
> *     you return with empty hands;*
> *In that place where fundamentally nothing is acquired,*
> *     you really acquire it.*

This verse reminds me of the years Charles and I lived on the Navajo reservation in Kaibeto, Arizona, where he worked as a teacher for the Bureau of Indian Affairs. David Monongye, an elder on the nearby Hopi reservation, used to invite us into the kiva for ceremonies the village Hoteville was having and then he would take us into his home afterward. I have always thought that one of the reasons we were welcome was because we went empty-handed. We didn't have any cameras, or tape recorders, or notebooks. We entered empty-handed and we left empty-handed. But what did we experience in David's presence, in that sacred space, that kept us coming back again and again?

Emptiness is not a thing, so nothing is acquired. In fact you lay down your load and experience a vast freedom. Emptying is an ongoing process. That's why you sit in meditation day after day. Thoughts, worries, and barriers can build with amazing speed, so you sit morning and evening and let them go. You lay them down again and again.

When you sit down in silence and let go of thoughts and barriers, nothing is denied or blocked from your awareness. When you let down your defenses, the energy used to hold your armor in place is mobilized for your use.

Some people describe the experience of emptiness as the collapse of the structure, like the roof and walls falling in. The collapse of the structure is the collapse of the ego and the collapse of a separate self. It is the collapse of the mental walls and barriers you have erected around yourself. With this collapse there is a sense of joy and liberation. You are free to be sensitive, compassionate, and alive. *Sunyata* is the Buddhist term for emptiness. A Zen verse says:

> *The spirit of* sunyata *is neither inside nor outside;*
> *Seeing, hearing, forms, and sounds are all empty.*

Empty of boundaries, there is no inside and outside; no subject and object; no self and other. Boundaries and categories can be useful, but if you cannot see beyond them, they block you from experiencing the unity, oneness, and wholeness of life. In transcending boundaries you are transformed and healed.

Often when we go on the road with Roshi Kennedy to help with Zen retreats it's like the circus coming to town. We arrive and have to set up the *zendo*, the Zen meditation room. A *zendo* is basically an empty room. So the first thing we do is move all the furniture out of a large hall. In the empty space we line up mats and cushions. Setting up a *zendo* is mostly a matter of emptying. Zen practice is mostly a matter of emptying too. Although this sounds quite austere, we can be encouraged by a Zen verse that reassures us:

> *If you want to reveal the sky, do not cover it up.*
> *It is empty, tranquil and originally bright.*

When you experience emptiness, you experience your essential nature that is tranquil and bright. You feel whole and at peace with the whole universe. This experience is deeply healing and it frees you and energizes you to help others find peace and healing.

# BEYOND SPEECH
# AND SILENCE:
## *What Is It?*

At times words are healing and at times silence is healing. But what is most healing of all is to experience what is beyond speech and silence.

Words, concepts, and thoughts divide reality into parts. In our minds reality is divided into objects that are placed into categories and given labels. Words, concepts, categories, and thoughts are necessary and useful in our everyday world. However, if that is our only way of experiencing reality, they become very limiting and distorting. In our culture, things are out of balance and many people live only in their heads. When you move beyond words and thoughts you expand your vision; experience new truths; live fully with body, mind, and spirit; and greatly enrich your life.

Excessive thought can bind you and blind you to the present moment. For example, sometimes when we are ill, rather than using our energy and resources to cope with the present reality, such as pain, nausea, or fatigue, we greatly add to our discomfort by worrying about what may happen next. We think, "Perhaps I will get worse." We worry about a long list of possible complications. We wonder how long it will be until we feel better. We worry that we may never feel good again. Yet most of the things we worry about never happen. Our excessive thoughts and worries needlessly add to our suffering. It is more effective to just stay in the present and deal with the situation immediately at hand.

Zen practice helps you learn to do this. During meditation you continuously choose to come back to an awareness of the present. This carries over into daily life. You learn to live out life fully moment to moment. Walking meditation is also good practice for life; just putting one foot in front of the other; taking one step at a time; being one with the ground beneath your feet, the sky above, and the people before and behind.

When you sit in meditation, you are silent and still and you allow your mind to settle down and become quiet. In the alert silence of meditation, you are able to perceive reality in a new way. In the wintertime, when a fresh blanket of snow has just covered the earth and there is deep stillness, you can directly experience "Silent night, holy night." In the silence, sometimes you hear a bird calling out in the snow. Birdsong ripples through your body like pure white snow. The moment is alive and vibrant.

Zen practice moves you beyond speech, beyond words, beyond thoughts, and beyond concepts to the direct experience of life lived fully in this moment. Once a monk came to Zen Master Joshu and asked him, "What is the meaning of the patriarch's coming from the West?" Joshu responded, "The oak tree in front of the garden." When the monk asked, "What is the meaning of the patriarch's coming from the West?" he was asking, "What is the essence of Zen?" When Joshu responded, "The oak tree in the front of the garden" he was not answering with a verbal explanation or description. Rather, he presented essential reality directly. He went beyond words to the fact, the direct experience of the oak tree in the present moment. Sitting in the cool refreshing shade of an oak tree on a hot summer afternoon you can appreciate the healing effect of Joshu's Zen.

It is said that many years later, after Joshu's death, a monk asked one of Joshu's students about his teacher's koan about an oak tree. To this inquiry Joshu's student replied, "My late master did not have any such koan. You should not abuse him." An oak tree is a perfect manifestation of essential nature, of the whole. The magnificence of an oak tree goes far beyond the words "oak tree." It was never Joshu's intention to convey the essence of Zen with words, but rather with the direct experience of the oak tree as not separate from the self or the rest of the universe.

There is an oak tree in my yard. It is growing in a stand of trees that was left undisturbed when the rest of the acre was bulldozed at the time the house was built. In the winter, it stands out because it holds on to some of its dried brown leaves when the rest of the trees are bare. You can experience an oak tree intimately, without stepping back into words. Look and see for yourself. What is an oak tree without the words, without the name?

Once a monk went to his teacher Vasumitra and said, "I have come to discuss the truth with you." Vasumitra said, "Good sir, if you discuss, it is not the truth; truth is not discussed." Discussion involves words and concepts that divide. Essential nature can be perceived directly, but it cannot be communicated through language that is dualistic. The minute we open our mouths to speak, we have stepped into the duality of subject and object, self and other, this and that.

Although Zen emphasizes the inadequacy of words, it also urges us not to get stuck in silence. What is there aside from speech and silence? A non-Buddhist once questioned the Buddha, "Aside from speech, aside from silence, what is it?" Buddha just sat there and the non-Buddhist suddenly understood. He thanked the Buddha profusely and went on his way. What did the non-Buddhist experience that satisfied his inquiring spirit and caused him to thank the Buddha so profusely? He directly experienced that the Buddha, he himself, and all things just as they are, are whole and complete and that neither speech nor silence can express it adequately.

Many years later a monk asked Zen Master Fuketsu how speech and silence are transcended. Fuketsu responded, "I constantly think of Konan in March where partridges chirp among hundreds of sweet-scented blossoms." In the direct experience of a fresh spring day, you are not separate, fragmented, or split by dualistic thoughts. You are whole and alive.

When I was in the hospital recovering from surgery my friends, family, and students sent me beautiful bouquets of flowers. There were hundreds of sweet-scented blossoms. The red of the roses, the pink of the carnations, the yellow of the lilies, and the white of the chrysanthemums sang out beyond speech and silence. Their silent songs were healing chants and prayers. Their fleeting, vibrant beauty kept me in touch with the fluid fragile beauty of life lived out moment by moment.

Some people seek out meditation because they long for silence and stillness. They do not realize that there is no silence apart from the sound. The silence is the sound. Likewise stillness moves in the fluidity of the moment. In meditation, even though you are sitting still, the muscles move to breathe in and out and the heart pumps to move blood to every cell in the body. There is no stillness apart from the movement. The stillness moves. To experience and live life beyond the duality of speech and silence, or stillness and movement, is a healing dance the whole universe joins in right now.

Once at a Zen retreat a woman came in to see me for an individual meeting. As she came through the door, I recognized her from the morning meditation period. She was an elegant older woman you couldn't help but notice. She was like an orchid that catches the eye with its graceful beauty. She sat down across from me and I was surprised when she said, "As a child, I was a shy little nothing of a girl. I was from a large family and no one ever noticed me. When I was in a room with other people, I was a wallflower. I always thought that if I closed my eyes, I would disappear." She went on to describe her experience during that morning's walking meditation. "As we walked silently along the hedgerow, I realized that I could not possibly disappear because I am not separate from the hedgerow, tall grasses, and trees." She said that with that realization she began to move confidently and finally had the feeling of fully joining in the great dance of life.

To move beyond speech and silence is a healing journey. It is not an external journey to some other place, nor is it an inner journey to some other state of consciousness. It is beyond external and internal. It is a journey that awakens you to right here and now. You awaken to the present moment, you experience the wholeness that is beyond dichotomies, and you see that there is nothing that you lack.

# JUST THIS:

## *A Life of Elegance*

When we experience wholeness, when we are healed, there is "just this." Just this fleeting moment alive and vibrant. Just this breath, in and out. Just this deep purple morning glory climbing up the railing, fresh and open in the foggy September dawn. Just this cup of coffee. Just this stack of papers needing to be sorted. Just this person standing before me torn open by grief. Just this highway crowded with eighteen-wheelers. Just myself, just as I am.

Beth, a woman I cared for after abdominal surgery, had several complications resulting in an extended hospital stay and much pain and discomfort. The surgeon made a mistake during her first surgery and a second surgery was required to correct it. Beth had practiced meditation for several years prior to her surgery. In addition to taking the pain medications that were prescribed for her, she noticed that if she did not fight the pain or separate herself from the pain by thinking about it, she could move with the sensations and she was much more comfortable. She moved with the sensations, just as they were, rather than trying to push them away or interpret the meaning of the sensations. Experiencing her pain as "just this" was healing for her and increased her level of comfort.

Sometimes pain is more overwhelming than this, and you groan or cry out despite pain medication and other comfort measures. Sometimes pain causes nausea and vomiting. At times like these, "just this" is groaning. "Just this" is crying out. "Just this" is vomiting. You do not add to the discomfort by thinking that you should be able to experience the pain differently; that you should not be groaning, crying out, or vomiting; or that in some way you are being punished. Rather you live out what is, just as it is.

The experience of "just this" does not only apply to a flower, a birdsong, a cup of tea, and all the beautiful aspects of life. It applies to your whole life, the happy times and the hard times. Nothing is excluded from your awareness. Your whole life is "just this" lived out fully moment by moment.

However "just this" does not mean just this as we ordinarily experience it. It does not mean objects perceived by and interacting with a subject. It does not mean artistically arranged objects in a still life painting. "Just this" is fluid. It is not an object or thing. It is experienced in the uniqueness of life as it is manifesting in each instant.

One day Zen Master Wu-kung asked Tien-tung, who had been his student for many years, "How do you see it these days?" Tien-tung replied, "Suppose I say that I am like this." Wu-kung did not approve of his answer and urged Tien-tung to go deeper and express what is beyond "like this." Tien-tung said that he could not express it in words and asked Wu-kung to express what is beyond. Wu-kung responded, "Suppose I say that I am not like this."

Tien-tung was awakened when he experienced "just

this" and "not just this" simultaneously. "Just this" is experienced moment to moment without trying to hold on to the experience and by not stepping back from the experience by thinking about it. When "just this" is experienced in this way, it is also "not just this." The vastness of the unknown is seen in the uniqueness of each creation.

The absolute reality of vast emptiness is experienced simultaneously with the relative realities of daily life. Two sutras that are chanted often in many Zen centers are "The Identity of the Relative and Absolute" and "The Heart Sutra." Both of these sutras emphasize that there is no separation between the bounded realities of everyday life and vast universal reality. In the words of "The Heart Sutra,"

> *Form is no other than emptiness,*
> *Emptiness is no other than form.*
> *Form is precisely emptiness,*
> *Emptiness is precisely form.*

When we lose separateness, we experience the whole of life in every moment and manifestation. There is nothing that exists elsewhere. There is nothing that you lack.

Sometimes this is described as the experience of thusness. Although we cannot find thusness through words, sometimes words can evoke the experience. The following Zen verse calls us to thusness:

> *If you wish to understand the meaning of this intimately,*
> *When is some seasoning not appropriate?*

The seasoning is the variety of life. We don't know the universal in some abstract way. Rather we find it in the intimacy of embracing each person, event, or thing. Seen in this light, each thing is radiant.

Such radiance can be seen clearly on a crisp autumn day, but it can also be experienced in the gray of winter with ice crystals on the window obscuring the vision. It can be seen in the darkness and in the light. It is experienced in each thing, just as it is.

There is a well-known koan titled, "Hyakujo and the Fox" about a priest named Hyakujo who made a mistake and as a result was reborn as a fox for five hundred lifetimes. Hyakujo believed that being reborn as a fox was a punishment for his mistake. This koan urges us to move beyond our fixed or erroneous ideas about mistakes and punishments. It does not deny that mistakes are made, and that sometimes there are grave consequences. However, it urges us not to limit ourselves to cause and effect thinking, but rather to expand our view to integrate an intuitive vision of the whole. In reference to this koan, Zen Master Mumon said, "If in regard to this you have the one eye, then you will understand that the former Hyakujo enjoyed five hundred lives of grace as a fox." Having the one eye means that you are able to see the universal in everything. You are able to see not only the dignity and elegance of the life of each human being, but also the dignity and elegance of all life forms.

One spring a mother fox gave birth to a litter of three fox cubs in a den in the side of the hill behind our house.

On the first warm days of spring the mother fox would sun herself on a large boulder beside the den while the cubs alternately nursed and frolicked in the tall grasses. Day after day I watched the fox care for her cubs with the sun glistening on her thick red coat. Is this scene the result of someone's past mistake or to be understood as some sort of punishment as was the case with Hyakujo? Or is it "just this," the elegant life of a fox?

Most people do not experience beautiful things as punishments, but they often think that they are being punished when pain or illness comes their way. Interpreting pain and illness as a punishment for some wrongdoing adds to a person's suffering. Helping the person move beyond this interpretation is a healing experience that brings increased comfort even in the midst of pain. Illness and pain are not punishments. They are "just this." The good times and the difficult times are both aspects of your whole elegant life.

# NONDUALITY:

## *There Is No Other*

Nonduality means no split or separation, a direct experience of the whole. These days, many people, on an intellectual level at least, have moved beyond dualistic thinking—especially when exploring the dichotomy between body and mind. Scientists have learned about the complex interrelationships between body and mind and have seen that we cannot separate the two. In this postmodern era, philosophers and scientists are moving beyond either/or thinking to both/and thinking. Rather than seeing things as opposite, we are able to view them as complements, as waves, or as patterns of the whole. Although this is a step in the right direction, an intellectual understanding of this is not enough. Healing comes when you directly experience nonduality.

Splitting or separating leaves you feeling broken, fragmented, pulled apart, isolated, and lonely; seeing and experiencing wholeness restores your vitality, energy, peace of mind, and feeling of unity with the whole universe. When we experience nonduality, even a major loss or illness falls within the context of wholeness. Even in the midst of illness, loss, or death, you can experience healing.

One day Zen Master Sanavasa asked a monk named Upagupta, "Did you make your home departure physically or in spirit?" Upagupta replied, "Truly, I made my home departure physically." Then Sanavasa asked, "How can the Wondrous Dharma of the Buddhas have anything to do with body or mind?" In an instant Upagupta saw beyond splits like physical or spiritual, body or mind. He directly experienced nonduality.

In Upagupta's time, over two thousand years ago, monks left their homes and entered a monastery so they could devote their lives to meditation. This was referred to as a physical home departure. Lay people who wanted to grow spiritually had to make time to meditate amid the demands of being householders. This was called making a home departure spiritually or mentally, since they remained at home physically.

This dichotomy between monastics and lay people has broken down in contemporary times. Often when I go to a Zen retreat, I sit together with monks, nuns, priests, and lay people. These are interesting times when monastics come out of the monasteries to attend retreats with lay people.

Why are we all drawn together to do this? We do this because Zen practice leads to a radical shift in perception—the direct experience of nonduality. Zen is not just a way to relax and appreciate life more. It is not just a way to work through your psychological problems. It opens you to the experience of wholeness.

The essence of the experience of nonduality is conveyed by the Zen verse:

*House demolished, the person perished,*
*neither inside nor outside,*
*Where can body and mind hide their forms?*

The phrase "house demolished" refers to the collapse of all mental constructs. All boundaries that separate are completely gone without a trace. Have you ever watched a heavy wrecking ball, suspended from a huge crane, swing and strike the side of an old building? The walls crumble and collapse completely in a cloud of dust. "The person perished" means that there is no separate self. Since there is no separate self, there is no other. All that I do, I do for the whole.

When you open yourself to the expanded vision of nonduality, you see that you are one with all the different people, animals, plants, mountains, rivers, and the great world. In the direct experience of nonduality, you swallow the whole universe. One day Zen Master Unmon held out his staff and said to the assembly of monks, "This staff has transformed itself into a dragon and swallowed up the universe! Where are the mountains, rivers, and the great world?" When you swallow the universe, you swallow the bad with the good. You see both the good and bad aspects of yourself. When you see your full capacity for good and bad, you experience that there is no other to blame. You don't deny how petty you can be therefore you are more likely to choose to be large.

When Zen masters speak of nonduality, they often

say, "Not one, not two." Not one means distinctions remain, and are appreciated more than ever. Not two means
you can, at the same time, experience the oneness or the
whole. This simultaneous experiencing of the universal
and each particular thing, frees you to act with the energy, power, and beauty of the whole.

When you experience nonduality, there are no boundaries and there is no inside and no outside. This is where
Zen differs from some other types of meditation. In some
meditation practices, you are instructed to close your
eyes and go deep within. You may be instructed to listen
to your inner voice. In Zen meditation, your eyes are
open. You sit in order to be awake and aware of what is
right here now.

In Zen meditation, rather than centering, you are
opening, expanding, letting go, emptying, and transcending the spatial distinctions between center and periphery. The distinctions like inside/outside and center/
periphery are useful in the relative realm of form and
phenomena, but they can become binders and blinders
that reinforce the sense of a separate self.

A Zen verse about the experience of nonduality says:

*There is no distinction or location, no edge or outside.*
*How could anything be larger than an autumn hair?*

Nonduality means that there are no boundaries whatsoever. Even the smallest thing like a tiny hair is one with
everything and is one with the whole. Each person, likewise, is not separate. You are one with everything and

one with the whole. This experience is vast and boundless like the sky.

In Christian terms, Jesus is speaking of nonduality when he says, "I and my Father are one." The pieces of communion bread are the body of Christ. At the same time, people reaching out to help others and the people they reach out to are the body of Christ. Mountains, trees, rivers, and oceans are also the body of Christ. It is all one body.

Rabbi Don Singer, who is also a Zen teacher, speaks movingly about the Jewish view of atonement. He points out that a broader interpretation of atonement includes not only guilt and forgiveness, but also an opening of your heart to the realization that you are "at-one" or one with everything. This insight eases your sorrow and fills you with wisdom and love.

One of the patients I helped care for was a young man whose arm was ripped off in a farm accident. He spent several days in the hospital while his shoulder was repaired surgically and then he was sent home. His wife was worried because during his hospital stay he received only physical care and no psychological counseling. She thought he would have great difficulty in adjusting to such a great loss and change in body image. She knew he needed more healing than just the physical healing of his shoulder.

Luckily a farmer from the community called and came to visit him. He was an older man who lost his leg in a farm accident. He invited the young man to come to a support group he belonged to for people who had experienced losses in serious farm accidents. The young man found that the support group was very healing for him. It helped him feel connected once again with himself, his family, his community, and the land he had worked for so many years. Although his arm was gone and greatly missed, he experienced that he was still whole.

Like Sanavasa who asked, "Did you make your home departure physically or in spirit?" you could ask, "Was the young man healed in body or mind?" Healing is not a matter of body or mind. It has to do with the whole and with your awareness and acceptance of your wholeness.

# BEING INCLUSIVE:
## Not Excluding Anything

Wholeness includes everyone and everything. All are welcome. Many people these days struggle with who they are and where they fit in. Many feel alienated and alone. A sense of belonging is a basic human need. With the experience of wholeness comes the healing experience of being united and feeling welcome and at home on the earth and in the universe.

Many of the Zen retreats and conferences I have attended have been aimed at interreligious dialogue. The participants have been Buddhist, Hindu, Jewish, Christian, and Moslem. These retreats and conferences were most successful when the participants spent a significant amount of their time together sitting in silent meditation. In the silence, the deep unity is directly experienced. As a result, the words and rituals we shared could be experienced more deeply, beautifully, and meaningfully.

During one interreligious retreat I attended, I went to the kitchen during one of the breaks to make bread for communion. While I was kneading, rolling, and shaping the bread, a young man came into the kitchen and sat down to watch me. After a while he said, "This bread is unleavened isn't it?" I replied. "Yes." He said, "The Jewish people ate unleavened bread during Passover." He went on to tell me that although he is now a Buddhist, his father was Jewish and his mother was Lutheran. He said that when he was growing up, he never really fit in either world and was teased in both. He said that the retreat was bringing it all together for him and he wasn't feeling conflict within himself. He said he felt more integrated and whole. So many young people today born to parents of different religions, cultures, and races need a way to embrace the differences and experience the unity.

Roshi Glassman, who has been a great leader in promoting interreligious dialogue, once shared from his experience of growing up Jewish that it is easier for a Jewish person to dialogue with a Buddhist than it is for an Orthodox Jew and a Reformed Jew to engage in dialogue with each other. Similarly, sometimes it is easier for Christians to dialogue with Buddhists than for Catholics and Protestants to engage in dialogue. It is time for us to transcend these boundaries and barriers and join together to work for the good of all people, animals, and the earth itself.

Culturally, Zen is inclusive. It started out with Buddha in India and was carried to China by Bodhidharma. In China aspects of Chinese thought and culture were integrated to create the Zen we know. From China it was carried on to Japan, Korea, and Vietnam. Now we are experiencing Zen in America with its own distinct flavor. In each geographic region and culture Zen has adapted, while maintaining its essence, and has integrated aspects of the culture, time, and place in which it was practiced and lived out.

People from diverse cultures and religions are not ex-

cluded and can benefit from practicing Zen. The koan
that makes this point most dramatically is titled "A
Non-Buddhist Questions the Buddha." In this koan a
non-Buddhist questions Buddha and quickly attains enlightenment. Ananda, who has been studying with Buddha for many years asks, "What did the non-Buddhist
realize that made him praise you so much?" Buddha
replied, "He is just like a fine horse that runs at the
shadow of a whip."

Ananda was the Buddha's cousin and it was said that
he remembered every word the Buddha ever taught. Yet
someone from a different family, who was not a Buddhist,
who was a newcomer and a stranger, was welcome to
come and study with Buddha. Not only that, but he gained
realization before Ananda did and was highly praised by
Buddha. You do not have to be a Buddhist for Zen practice to expand your vision. Everyone is welcome to give
it a try.

Being inclusive does not ignore the differences. Zen
includes both oneness and differences at the same time. A
Zen verse about oneness and difference says:

> With realization, all things are of one family,
> Without realization, everything is separate and different.
> Without realization, all things are of one family,
> With realization, everything is separate and different.

Realization is the simultaneous experience of unity and
diversity, of the universal and the particular.

As a woman, I was deeply moved when I became a

Zen teacher. There are still so many religions and denominations that don't allow women to assume positions of leadership. In the Zen hall, men and women sit side by side, enriched by our differences and by what we share in common as human beings.

Recently I was discussing cultural sensitivity with the nursing students I teach. One student shared that her father was in the service. When he was stationed in Hawaii, she and her brothers experienced firsthand what it is like to be a minority. Because they were white, the Asian majority rejected them. She said it was so hard that they had to transfer to private school. As the discussion continued, other students in the class shared that they were from small towns nearby and that they were embarrassed that their high schools, communities, and churches shunned people from different races and from the North. One African-American student thanked the class because she had been fearful and worried about coming down from Maryland to southwest Virginia to go to nursing school, but she was greatly relieved and grateful that all of the students in the class had been entirely kind, accepting, and welcoming to her.

There is a great need in our world for openness, acceptance, inclusiveness, and warm welcome. Zen cultivates a wide and open mind that can bring together people from diverse nations, races, cultures, religions, and genders. Zen masters sometimes call this Big Mind. When we open ourselves to the expanded vision of Big Mind, we see that we are one with all the different people, animals, plants, mountains, rivers, and the whole universe.

From a Zen perspective Big Mind includes everything, even seeming contradictions. Rather than limiting ourselves to either/or we expand to include both/and. Whitman expressed this expanded vision in his poetry:

> *Do I contradict myself?*
> *Very well then I contradict myself,*
> *(I am large, I contain multitudes.)*

The expanded vision of wholeness transcends dualistic opposition and includes everything.

When we open ourselves to the whole we see and acknowledge both good and bad aspects. Included in our experience are both the joy and the pain. In his book, *Nine-Headed Dragon River*, Roshi Matthiessen described the experience he had caring for his wife Deborah while she was in the hospital dying of cancer. By the time Christmas arrived, Deborah was too ill to leave the hospital so several of her friends came to her room with special food and gifts. Deborah sat up in bed and thoroughly enjoyed the party. As Roshi Matthiessen participated in the festivities, he thought, "Under the covers, Ho Ko (Deborah) was already an old woman, her hips and beautiful legs collapsed, black and blue from needles, but she was still lovely when propped up in bed, and she wore her *rakusu* like a proud child. I watched our friends' faces admiring the brave, calm, smiling woman in the bed. I admired her, too, putting out of my mind those other days when her dying was neither calm nor lovely, those days no one knew about but the nurses and me."

As a nurse, this passage is especially meaningful to me. The husband and nurses saw the whole experience of illness, the good days and the bad, the beauty and the horror, the courage and the anguish. Being inclusive means being with another human being through the whole experience of illness, no matter how difficult; to comfort and care for him or her to the end. You come face to face with what is and do not turn away. You see that life includes death.

# SPIRITUALITY:
## The Mystery and Wonder of Life

Healing is not just physical and psychological; it is also spiritual. People define the term spirituality in many different ways. What most of these definitions have in common is that spirituality has to do with the essence and meaning of life. Spirituality influences values and how your life is lived; it opens you to the mystery and wonder of life and fills you with energy and vitality. Spirituality results in a deep sense of connection with people, all creatures, and the earth. Spiritual development manifests in love and compassionate action.

For many years spirituality was not mentioned in the medical setting and especially not in the psychiatric setting. There was a great split between science and religion. This schism was even greater in the psychiatric setting partly due to Freud's tremendous influence on the discipline. It is only in recent years that the word spirituality is being heard in medical and psychiatric settings. This is in part due to the work of physicians such as Herbert Benson, Dean Ornish, and M. Scott Peck and nurses such as Barbara Dossey, Jean Watson, and Janet Quinn. Respected institutions like Harvard Medical School now regularly sponsor conferences on "Spirituality and Medicine." The importance of spirituality in healing is beginning to be acknowledged.

Spirituality is healing because it opens your eyes to the broader picture and you see that you are whole. You are a body-mind-spirit whole. Sometimes medical care is viewed in a mechanical manner. When you are ill you go to the hospital and the broken part is repaired. But human beings are not machines. In addition to physical care, our psychological and spiritual nature needs to be taken into consideration. In nursing even physical care needs to be provided in a way that respects a person's humanity. This is conveyed by the way a nurse touches, speaks, listens, relates, and attends. It is communicated by the nurse's presence and her or his competent, compassionate action.

Zen is a spiritual practice. It opens you to the direct experience of wholeness and heals you from the sense of isolation and alienation so widespread in our society. It reconnects you with yourself, other people, and all of creation. It rekindles your sense of wonder and communion with mystery.

Some people do Zen mediation or other kinds of meditation for the physical benefits. For example, meditation can be used as a relaxation technique to lower blood pressure, slow the heart rate, and decrease the respiratory rate. The posture of Zen meditation is healthful and tends to carry over and improve posture throughout the day. However, Zen meditation is so much more than a relaxation technique or a way to improve posture.

Some people are attracted to Zen and other kinds of meditation because of the psychological benefits. Zen meditation disciplines and calms the mind. Sitting silently in meditation you become aware of how your mind works. You see the same thoughts arise over and over again. You become very familiar with them and eventually tire of them. The thoughts lose their grip and you are able to let go of them. This process applies to feelings and emotions as well. However, Zen practice is more than a way to calm and ease your mind.

Zen practice cannot be explained strictly in physical terms. Nor can it be explained entirely using psychological terms. It extends beyond the physical and psychological into the spiritual realm. The following Zen verse alludes to the spiritual nature of Zen:

> *Extremely fine subtle consciousness is not*
> *emotional attachment;*
> *It constantly makes That One preach keenly.*

Spirituality is subtler than thoughts and emotions. It deals with an awareness or consciousness that is beyond words and feelings. Although Zen does not address the issue of whether or not there is a God, throughout the *Denkoroku,* a classic collection of Zen koans, language such as "That One" and "The Old Fellow" is used. At the same time, there is an emphasis placed on not conceptualizing ultimate reality in any way. Therefore, we cannot name it, make it into a thing, or say anything about it. It is mystery. It is beyond our human imagination. It cannot be said to exist or not exist. It is not a thing.

Spiritual knowledge requires a different way of understanding than the scientific knowledge we are used to from years of school. Willis Harman describes an extended science that has four levels. The most basic level includes the physical sciences like physics and chemistry. The next level is the biological sciences. The third level is the psychological and the fourth is the spiritual. Physics and chemistry cannot explain all of the processes occurring in living systems, so we must step up to the biological level for explanations and understanding. In a similar manner, human behavior and feelings cannot be explained using biological principles alone, so we step up to the psychological level. Spirituality cannot be entirely explained using knowledge from the field of psychology, so we step up to the spiritual level. Each level contains and transcends the previous levels. Harman also describes the ways knowledge is developed and validated in each level. He states that the monasteries of the major world religions down through the ages are the laboratories for experiencing, developing, and validating spiritual knowledge.

Spiritual knowing is not limited to traditional scientific ways of knowing. In fact, Zen masters call it "not knowing" and it is this kind of knowing that is needed for us to experience the whole. The following Zen verse gives advice on seeking spiritual knowledge:

> *Avoid seeking Him in someone else*
> *Or you will be far apart from the Self.*
> *Solitary now am I, and independent,*
> *But I meet Him everywhere.*
> *He now is surely me,*

*But I am not Him.*
*Understanding it in this way,*
*You will be directly one with thusness.*

Spiritual knowledge is not sought somewhere else, but rather through studying the self. You will come to see that the self is everything throughout the universe. Realization is the experience of unity with everything—even with distinction and diversity.

Though spiritual experience transcends religious differences, these differences remain. When we experience unity or oneness, we feel a sense of reverence, awe, and gratitude and are deeply grateful to the tradition of teachers who developed and handed down Zen over the course of twenty-five hundred years. At the same time we appreciate the truth and beauty contained in the diverse religious traditions of the world.

Zen Master Dogen had his great awakening when his teacher Ju-ching said, "Studying Zen is the dropping off of body and mind." When Dogen heard this he moved beyond body and mind and experienced the spiritual. Although the spiritual realm transcends body and mind, at the same time, body and mind are nothing other than spiritual. They are doors to spiritual experience. Our posture and breathing are spirit. Our mind is spirit, is Big Mind, or No Mind. We come to see that everything around us is spirit and the earth beneath our feet is holy ground.

Although widespread interest in the relationship between spirituality and healing has been a recent phenomenon, for many years the effectiveness of Alcoholics Anonymous (AA) in treating addiction to alcohol has demonstrated the power of this relationship. Through participation in AA, alcoholics use and develop their spiritual resources to maintain sobriety and revitalize their lives. A Cherokee man named Roy who I took care of in the hospital told me that he was very active in AA and that in fact it had saved his life. He pulled a chip from his pocket and proudly showed it to me. On one side it said, "Native American in Recovery." On the other side was the following prayer:

> *Oh Great Spirit, whose voice I hear in the wind,*
> *Whose breath gives life to the world,*
> *Hear me, I come to you as one of your many children.*
> *I am small and weak.*
> *I need your strength and wisdom.*
> *May I walk in beauty.*

Roy said he tries to help other people and that helps him stay sober. He is an AA sponsor and he serves as the leader of a local club for Cherokee young people that teaches them the stories, songs, dances, and ways of their culture. He said that in some tribes the people do not remember their culture, so the members of those tribes imitate the Cherokee, Sioux, and Navajo ways. But these are not their ways. He said, "If they pray, their ways will come back. If they really pray."

Zen meditation can be viewed as wordless prayer. It is not a means to an end. It is simply being with what is already here. Sitting in silence you become aware that you are already whole. You see that you are one with the whole and this opens you to the unknown, to vastness, to diversity, and to limitless possibilities. You experience healing. Your spirit is renewed and you are brought back into harmony. In gratitude you reach out to heal others and to heal the earth.

# SUFFERING:

## *Letting Go*

Serving as a caregiver has its roots in the intention to alleviate suffering. Buddha delineated six types of suffering that people experience over the course of their lives—the trauma of birth and disease, the losses that come with old age, death, being tied to what you dislike, and being separated from what you love. Buddha taught that the cause of suffering is selfish craving and the end of suffering is found in letting go of selfish craving.

While caring for people who are seriously ill and dying, I see that there are indeed many types of suffering. Some people tell me that death is not the worst thing. There are things worse than death. For some the worst thing is pain. For some the worst thing is struggling to clear their airway to take the next breath. For some it is financial concerns—that they will run out of money or use up all the money that their families need. For some it is not being able to care for their young children. For some it is dying when they hadn't really been alive. They regret not having been truly present and missing the opportunity to be intimate with family and friends.

For some of these people living each day to the fullest becomes their goal and their joy. They come face to face with life and death and respond with the whole of their being. We can learn important lessons about living from people who are seriously ill or dying. We do not take suffering lightly. We live it and learn from it. Life and death go hand and hand.

Sometimes in the evening at a Zen retreat you will hear the following chant coming out of the silence:

> *Let me respectfully remind you:*
> *Life and death are of supreme importance;*
> *Time passes swiftly by and opportunity is lost.*
> *Each of us must strive to awaken.*
> *Awaken! Take heed!*
> *Do not squander your life!*

This chant urges you to wake up and to take advantage of each moment of your life whatever your circumstances. It is a reminder of impermanence and the fleeting, ever-changing nature of life. This brings comfort in the knowledge that the hard times will pass, yet also grief in the passing of the people and things you love. It attunes you to the fact that this moment is the only moment you have.

When his cancer was advancing, Suzuki Roshi tried to prepare his students for the time when he would die by saying, "If when I die, the moment I'm dying, if I suffer that is all right, you know; that is suffering Buddha." He did not deny that suffering is a part of life or that he might suffer. Instead, he accepted life and lived each experience as it came his way. The expectation that you "will not" or "should not" suffer multiplies your suffering.

Many years ago in China, Hui-ko longed to study

with Zen Master Bodhidharma, but when he got to the monastery Bodhidharma would not let him enter. To demonstrate the seriousness of his intent to study Zen, Hui-ko stood outside Bodhidharma's window all night in the falling snow until the snow was up to his waist. The next morning when Bodhidharma saw him, he still would not let him enter, so Hui-ko cut off his left arm with a sword. When Bodhidharma saw this he finally let him in and accepted him as his student.

Of course, this story is not to be taken literally—it certainly does not advocate or glorify cutting off any limbs. Instead, this graphic imagery illustrates the difficult choices, the pain, and the sacrifice inherent not only in life, but in the pursuit of a deep spiritual path. We don't have to create or search for sacrifices. They will come our way in ways that are unique for each of us.

After Hui-ko finally got in to study with Bodhidharma, one day he told him: "I have already put an end to all conditions." Bodhidharma asked, "Doesn't that result in death?" Hui-ko replied, "It does not result in death." "What is your proof?" asked Bodhidharma. "I am always clearly aware." replied Hui-ko.

When Hui-ko said that he had put an end to all conditions, he was referring to letting go of selfish craving, letting go of thoughts and theories, letting go of expectations, letting go of controlling, letting go of fixed opinions, and letting go of a separate self. The process of letting go can be difficult and at times it can feel like death, but it does not result in death. Letting go opens you to new life—a life of clear awareness of the whole.

In Zen literature the sword is a symbol of cutting off and of letting go. The *kyosaku* stick sometimes used in the Zen hall is a symbol of the sword of Manjushri. It is the sword of compassion that cuts off daydreaming and delusions and brings you into the present moment. The sting on your shoulders wakes you up and others in the hall hearing the *whack* wake up too. Zen pushes you to cut off preoccupation and mental commentary that separate you from life itself.

Zen practice is not about avoiding the difficult aspects of life. It is about clearly seeing all aspects of life, the whole thing. In Zen, we do not avoid or escape suffering, but rather let go so we can see it and see beyond it. Zen brings you face to face, and eyebrow to eyebrow, with life's difficulties, complexities, pain, beauty, and joy. It is about waking up and living life completely in both happy times and sad.

In her little meditation room at home, Roshi Richardson has a statue of Mary holding her dead son Jesus. She says that for her it is an image of letting go. It represents the radical letting go of everything, the emptying that is essential in Zen practice. Mary has arms that hold, but do not cling. She is a nurturing presence that does not constrict. It is especially difficult to let go of your own child.

Recently I took care of a young man who has schizophrenia. He lives in a cave in the woods on the edge of town. He went to visit his mother and she could see that he needed help so she talked him into going to the hospital. As she was driving him there he changed his mind and when they stopped at a stop sign, he jumped out of the car and ran into the woods. He said that for a long time he sat in his hiding place in the trees and watched the police and his mother looking for him. Eventually, she gave up the search and went home. Sometimes we have no choice but to let go. A few days later, the young man walked back into town and checked himself into the hospital.

The other day I took care of a seventy-eight-year-old woman who was in the hospital after having a stroke. As I was cleaning and diapering her and helping her get dressed, she was crying. She was crying because she was being discharged from the hospital that day, but was not returning to her home. She was no longer able to take care of herself so she was going to live in a nursing home. She said she was a nurse herself and for more than fifty years she took care of other people. Now she needed other people to take care of her. In her tears, I could see her suffering and how difficult letting go can be.

Although letting go can be very difficult, when you stop clinging to the past or to how you would like things to be, you free yourself to live life fully just as it is. Experiencing the fullness of life in the present, even amid difficult circumstances, brings a sense of wholeness and healing to your life. When you experience the healing power of letting go, you can share what you have learned to help others let go and heal.

# ACCEPTANCE:

## Things Just as They Are

As you practice acceptance, you grow in your ability to face and fully accept people, circumstances, and things just as they are. Acceptance is not a passive resignation to circumstances and situations. Acceptance is not just making the best of a bad situation. It is an active presence to life just as it is. Acceptance means not pushing away, denying, or excluding things or circumstances that you do not like. It is the process of continually dropping expectations and judgments and accepting what is. Acceptance expands your vision, acknowledging all aspects of yourself and the world. Nothing is walled off. Total acceptance connects you with everything and helps you experience wholeness.

Acceptance takes place in the present moment. You remain right here and now dealing with what is. Your energy is not going into thinking about what might have been or wishing things were different. Your energy is available to respond most effectively to the situation at hand. We generally don't have a problem accepting good things. It is the bad things that challenge our ability to accept things as they are. Acceptance is the process of transcending good and bad, of transcending duality. Acceptance is transformative and frees us to be a healing presence in the world.

There is a Zen koan about a woman who is deep in meditation near the throne of Buddha. A great bodhisattva, Manjusri, representing oneness, snaps his fingers trying to awaken her, but he cannot. A less advanced, beginner bodhisattva named Momyo, snaps his fingers and the woman is immediately awakened. One point this koan is making is that the oneness of all phenomena is manifested in and experienced through the differences of relative existence. Momyo represents differentiation— that is why he is able to awaken the woman. This is expressed powerfully in the verse:

> *One can awaken the woman, the other cannot;*
> *Both have their own freedom.*
> *On one occasion a god-mask appears, on another*
>     *a devil-mask;*
> *Even in failure, an elegant performance.*

This verse urges us to move beyond good and bad to perceive and accept the underlying unity manifested in all things both good and bad.

This koan came to life for me one day when I was taking care of a young man named Jeff who has schizophrenia. When he was very ill he would swear at me calling me a bitch and a whore. If I got too close to him when bringing him his meals or his medication, he would try to hit or kick me. On several occasions he needed to be in four-point restraint to keep him from harming himself or someone else. It took many months to find a medication that helped him. One evening when he was recovering, the nursing staff and recreation therapist took the patients on an outing to a concert. The performer was a musician both the patient and I had admired for many years. We had a wonderful time at the concert clapping, cheering, and moving to the music. All evening Jeff's sensitive, caring, human side shined through. The phrase from this verse, "On one occasion a god-mask appears, on another a devil-mask" drifted through my mind. I took care of Jeff during many subsequent relapses. Totally accepting him and his current condition, and providing the best care possible, was an elegant performance in both the difficult times when the medications failed to help and in the good times when he regained his ability to function in this world.

There is a prayer about acceptance that is frequently prayed at Alcoholics Anonymous meetings:

> *God, grant me the serenity*
> *to accept the things*
> *I cannot change,*
> *Courage to change the*
> *things I can, and the*
> *wisdom to know the difference.*

This prayer is an acknowledgment that you cannot control all aspects of your own life, the lives of others, or the world at large. You are not in control. This realization can be frightening, but the acceptance of it can be liberating. Accepting the fact that you are not in control of many things does not eliminate your responsibility to work toward positive change. This is also a prayer for wisdom because it is not always easy to discern what you can change in a positive way and how best to accomplish it. Overall this is a prayer for the serenity and equanimity that flow from the acceptance of yourself, your strengths, your responsibilities, your limitations, and your life just as it is.

One day Zen Master Gettan asked a monk who was studying with him, "Keichu made a hundred carts. If he took off both wheels and removed the axle, what would he make clear about the cart?" This koan reminds me of one of my favorite episodes in the old television series, *Superman*. In this episode Jimmy Olsen was driving down a steep, twisting mountain road at high speed in a convertible. The steering wheel came loose and Jimmy Olsen was frantically turning it in the air while the car sped on down the mountainside out of control. When things fall apart you are directly confronted with the fact that you are not in control. Roshi Kennedy once said in reference to this koan, "If this is not frightening to you, you haven't gone deep enough." Fear also must be accepted as part of the human condition. This koan asks you to take a look at what acceptance of all the parts teaches you about the whole.

Not controlling can also be viewed as not grasping or not clinging. We try to maintain control to keep bad things from happening, and to keep ourselves from losing people or things we love. A controlling, clinging kind of love can be stifling and can destroy a relationship.

Love that accepts the other just as they are creates an atmosphere in which a person can grow and blossom. This acceptance includes embracing life's inevitable changes. Thus our appreciation of the people and things we love and enjoy heightens, because we realize they are only present to us in this fleeting moment of time. We must wake up and be present to them right here and now just as they are.

A friend of mine was upset because despite her best efforts her eight-year-old son, Brian, who had been frequently in trouble, was expelled from school. She and her husband had worked closely with the school and with a child psychiatrist and it was determined that Brian had attention deficit hyperactivity disorder. Although Brian's parents were well aware of his dangerous and disruptive behavior both at home and at school, it was hard for them to accept his diagnosis and his need to take medication regularly. Over time, they saw that the medication was necessary so he could remain safe, stay in school, learn to read, and make friends among the other children. Through all Brian's ups and downs, his parents loved him, got him the help he needed, and accepted him with both his strengths and limitations. This helped both Brian and his parents adjust and heal.

There was once a very old Zen master named Tokusan. One day he came down to the dining hall carrying his bowls. A young monk named Seppo saw him and asked him why he was coming down to eat when the lunch bell had not rung yet. Without saying anything

Tokusan turned around and returned to his room. In this scene, perhaps Master Tokusan has grown old and has become a little forgetful and confused. Seppo does not accept old Tokusan just as he is. He does not appreciate the beauty of the old man coming down to lunch a little too early. He misses the opportunity to greet the old man warmly and offer him a drink, a snack, and a little conversation to hold him over until lunch is ready. Instead, Seppo jumps on the opportunity to correct old Tokusan. But Tokusan is wise. He realizes that Seppo's rate of growth, spiritual development, and insight cannot be forced or rushed. He knows it takes time for fruit to ripen and he is patient with Seppo and accepts him just as he is. Tokusan simply turns and goes back to his room.

Some have called Zen meditation a form of prayer. If so, it is a very open-ended form of prayer, a kind of prayerfulness. There is no expectation of any result or of any particular outcome. There is no image or idea of who is praying or who is being prayed to. It is as open-ended and accepting as Jesus' prayer, "Thy will be done." A friend from Iran told me that in the Moslem tradition there is a similar prayer, "Enshallah"—"If it is the will of God." These prayers open us to an attitude of acceptance of life as it unfolds.

Acceptance brings us to a fuller appreciation of life just as it is. Sometimes we add to our sorrow by dwelling on how we think life should be rather than living it out fully just as it is. One woman I worked with was sad and depressed because her husband had recently died and she felt very lonely. As the holiday season was approaching, she found herself becoming increasingly sad and depressed because Christmas was not going to be the way she wished it to be or the way she thought it should be. Her only son was going to be out of town visiting his wife's family and she would be home alone. She made plans to go to church and have dinner with friends on Christmas Eve. She decided to spend Christmas Day at home. She curled up on the sofa beneath a warm comforter, sipped cups of hot tea, and read a good book from cover to cover without interruption. Rather than thinking about what Christmas Day was supposed to be, she said she accepted and enjoyed the day just as it was. She said it was a good and peaceful Christmas Day.

Acceptance of yourself, your circumstances, and your responsibilities has a healing effect on your life. Acceptance of others helps them feel truly loved and cared for. In an atmosphere of being accepted just as they are, they can flourish and grow to be the best human beings they can be.

# BALANCE:

## *Integrating Opposites*

Working as a nurse taking care of several patients at the same time, often I feel like a juggler spinning plates. I run from plate to plate, giving each a spin before it loses momentum and falls to the floor breaking into a hundred pieces. Many nurses are master jugglers. In some ways they are highly balanced and integrated. They integrate human warmth and caring with technical competence and scientific knowledge. However, in a very basic way, many of us are unbalanced. We meet the needs of others but ignore our own needs, often working for hours without a break. In the long run working without a break and not meeting your own needs leads to exhaustion, burnout, and illness. In order to heal others you must experience healing yourself. Balancing work and play, self and other, rest and activity, eating and exercising, and body and spirit, restores the capacity to heal and be whole.

Gary, a man I once took care of, owned a successful company. He worked long hours and ate out often. He was making lots of money and was on the run until he had a heart attack at age forty-eight. After coronary bypass surgery he enrolled in a cardiac rehabilitation program. He was faced with the need to make changes in the way he was living his life. He learned new ways of eating that not only decreased his fat intake, but also increased the amount of time he spent at home preparing food and eating meals with his family. He started taking a half hour walk outdoors each day and felt a renewed connection with nature. Fishing was Gary's form of relaxation and contemplation. On Saturday mornings he sat on the riverbank and fished in the peace of the nearby forest. Several months after his surgery he said that although the experience was extremely difficult for him, it woke him up and helped him bring his life back into balance.

Not only do you need to balance and meet your physical needs, but you also need to balance and meet your psychological needs. Cindy, a woman I took care of recently, suffered from depression. One day she took a nap after lunch and as she was resting in bed she had a dream. The dream gave her insight into why she was feeling so depressed. In her mind's eye she saw two children playing. One child rode on a red scooter over and over again while the other child never got a turn. Finally, the child who stood waiting for her turn said, "If I'm never going to get a turn, I don't want to play anymore." When she heard the child speak, she recognized her own voice. Hearing her own voice had a dramatic impact on her. She said she realized that some people need to learn to share and give others a turn or people won't want to play with them anymore. Others, like herself, needed to learn to take a turn. She said, "It sounds really simple. Even little children know about taking turns. Why did it take me so long to wake up?" She had put so much of her time and energy into meeting the needs of her family that her own needs had gone unmet. She started taking a turn and little by little she balanced meeting the needs of others with meeting her own needs.

Zen practice brings balance to life. Basic balance and sanity are restored. But the balance I am speaking of does not mean maintaining the status quo or not rocking the boat. Rather the balance cultivated by Zen practice is dynamic. It is the total awareness in the present moment that is required to walk the razor's edge. It is the ability to experience the full range of phenomena and to integrate extremes to enrich your life. Balance is the profound ability to integrate opposites.

For example, when you sit in Zen meditation you practice balance. While sitting, your spine is straight but not rigid. It is flexible and balanced. Maintaining a comfortable, erect posture during meditation is a matter of making subtle adjustments of your position to find just the right balance. You are both disciplined and relaxed at the same time. The mind is alert but not strained. In this balanced state of body and mind you are prepared to see and integrate whatever arises. You can experience both the wonderful and the horrible without the need to deny or wall off. The balance and flexibility that you practice during meditation allow you to go out into life and stand in the wind without getting knocked over.

We live in a very fast-paced, materialistic, high-tech society. It's hard to know how to operate the computer, answering machine, stove, or VCR without sitting down for hours to read the instruction manuals. Often we are confronted with complicated insurance and income tax forms. Zen meditation is a refreshing way to sit still, be silent, and allow your body, mind, and spirit to heal by providing a natural balance to the noise, clutter, and information that bombard you daily. It is a way to step back and experience another side of life.

Buddha experienced the need for balance in life and called the path he eventually came to the Middle Way. For a time he was too ascetic in his approach to meditation, fasting and depriving himself of sleep. He became ill and was not able to continue his meditation practice. He found that it was better to take the middle ground, neither eating nor sleeping too much or too little.

Many people have a hard time finding balance in their lives with all the demands at work and at home. Many young parents ask me, "How do you balance work responsibilities and spending time with the children with a meditation practice?" It is a delicate balance that requires you to simplify your life and determine what is most important to you. Zen takes regular daily practice. For most parents, early morning before the children get up is the best time to sit silently in meditation, and then again in the evening after the children go to sleep. Twenty-five minutes morning and evening is a good amount of daily practice, but if this is not possible, fifteen minutes every day is better than sporadic practice or giving up entirely. Daily practice is deepened by periodically attending retreats. Couples need to be creative and flexible, sometimes taking turns, in supporting each other's practice while giving the children the attention they need.

Sometimes in the course of your life you may find that your life has become unbalanced and you find yourself exhausted, run-down, or ill. This is the time to stop and take a look at your life—to consider what is most meaningful to you and where your life can be simplified. You need to take time to rest and focus on getting well. You may need to bring your family life back into balance by paying more attention to your loved ones or by expressing your affection and appreciation for them.

It is not easy to find a balance between conflicting demands. There are needs for independence and needs for dependence; for individuation and connection; our own needs and the needs of others; the need for excitement and the need for security; to be rational and to be intuitive; for solitude and for companionship. Zen meditation can move you beyond duality to see all of these needs as facets of the whole. This insight integrates your life and restores a dynamic sense of balance. You don't view life in terms of either/or but rather both/and. Opposing needs are not seen as opposites, but rather as complements. The experience of nonduality, wholeness, or oneness integrates and balances. At the same time the diversity of multiple needs and demands remains. It is the delicate balance between "not one and not two."

The dynamic balance of Zen is conveyed in the following verse:

*Walking on the edge of a sword,*
*Running over a ridge of jagged ice;*
*Not using steps or ladders,*
*Jumping from the cliff with hands free.*

This verse describes the keen sense that allows us to walk on the razor's edge, balancing beyond opposites. When we transcend the linear logic that categorizes, separates, and isolates, life becomes fluid and fully integrated. Making a great leap we experience wholeness all at once in the present moment with no steps or stages on the way. Without clinging to extremes, or holding on to dichotomies, our hands are extended freely.

This is like the dramatic leap that occurs when a woman becomes a mother for the first time. Although she plans and prepares for the birth of her baby, she cannot know how her life will be transformed. Often I have watched as a new mother holds her baby for the first time. You can see the change come over her face as she looks into the baby's eyes and the baby returns her gaze. Immediately, she transcends the dichotomy between self and other. Mother and baby are "not one and not two." The mother steps forward into a new role that requires delicately balancing her needs and the needs of the infant she holds in her arms.

The balance of Zen is like the balance used in surfing. You move with and ride the waves of life. Sitting in meditation you are aware of the highs and lows of life and that your thoughts and emotions are constantly changing. Zen practice does not eliminate your emotional swings, but rather teaches you how to maintain your balance, move with them, and ride them out. The well-known verse from Ecclesiastes tells us that for everything there is a season:

> *A time for tears,*
> *a time for laughter:*
> *a time for mourning,*
> *a time for dancing.*
> *A time for throwing stones away,*
> *a time for gathering them up;*
> *a time for embracing,*
> *a time to refrain from embracing.*

We move through each season living it fully. Balance frees us to respond with all our resources to each experience as it arises and then move on to experience what the next moment brings.

# RIGHT HERE:
## *Transcending Space*

Healing takes place right here in the present moment. Where else could you possibly be? There is a human tendency to look somewhere else or to wish you were somewhere else. You think the grass is greener on the other side of the fence. You think happiness can be found somewhere over the rainbow, but like Dorothy you may come to find that happiness awaits you right in your own backyard. You can find peace and experience wholeness right where you are.

A young man named William I've taken care of on and off for a number of years has schizophrenia and lives in a cardboard box under a bridge. When life in the street gets too rough and someone beats him up, or when he gets too sick, he ends up back in the hospital for a while. During his most recent hospital stay, I asked him, "What brought you back into the hospital this time?" He said, "They dropped me out of an airplane onto the roof of the hospital."

William's mother died about a year ago and the home he lived in while he was growing up was sold. From time to time the family who lives there now wakes up and finds him sleeping on the lawn. This time, the family living in his old home called the police and William asked the police to bring him to the hospital. As I admitted him and showed him around the unit, he told me he was exhausted and hadn't slept in days. He said, "There's nowhere safe for me to sleep anymore." I showed him his room and his bed and reassured him, "You're safe here with us. You can sleep right here." He climbed into bed and fell sound asleep. As a caregiver it is important to be welcoming and to create an environment where healing can take place. A person must feel safe to heal right here and now.

Once a monk asked Zen Master Kempo, "In a sutra it says, 'Ten-direction Bhagavats, one Way to the gate of nirvana.' I wonder where the Way is." Kempo lifted up his stick, drew a line in the air, and said, "It is right here."

The monk read in a sutra that for all the Buddhas there is only one Way to enlightenment and he asked where is this one Way. Kempo responded that everyone and everything is already walking on the one Way. There is no need to look elsewhere for it. The Way is always right here in each place you are and in each action you do.

My husband Charles and I have traveled thousands and thousands of miles studying Zen. Our Zen teacher Roshi Kennedy lives over five hundred miles away in Jersey City. We've spent so much time going back and forth to Zen retreats in New York on Interstate 81 that I jokingly call our practice interstate Zen. Often for us Interstate 81 is the Way. During long hours of driving, I console myself with the fact that New York is a lot closer than Japan. Down through the ages, people traveled long distances on foot or by boat, like Bodhidharma and other monks like him who carried Zen from India to China.

Zen Master Dogen traveled to China to study Zen and bring it back to Japan. In our time many Zen teachers and Zen students traveled back and forth from Japan to America. Sometimes it takes a lot of travel to be right here.

When Zen Master Kempo responded to the monk's question he held up his stick. Zen teachers have a stick that they use in teaching called a teaching stick. When Charles and I became Zen teachers, rather than getting sticks from Japan, Roshi Kennedy suggested that perhaps we would like sticks from this country, something that was particularly meaningful to us. Charles went out into the woods near our home and found two saplings that had grown in a twisted formation from honeysuckle vines wrapping around them. From these he cut and polished our teaching sticks. Coming from this soil, they are a symbol of Zen traveling across great distances and taking root here in America.

Ejo studied with Zen Master Dogen for many years and one day he heard the phrase, "a single hair pierces many holes." Hearing this Ejo was suddenly awakened and expressed his insight in a verse:

*Space, from the beginning, has not admitted even a needle;*
*Vast, nonreliant, it is beyond all discussion.*
*Do not say that a hair passes through the many holes;*
*Empty and spotless, it is unmarked by any scars.*

In his direct experience of emptiness or essential nature, Ejo saw that a tiny hair is emptiness, and that in its emptiness it is one with everything. Its essential nature is one with the essential nature of the whole universe. The realm of emptiness is beyond space and time. In its emptiness the tiny hair occupies no space and pierces no holes. There is no distance between the hair and the hole. Emptiness cannot be pierced by emptiness. As the verse emphasizes, this is beyond discussion. It cannot be described, but it can be directly experienced. In rare instances this insight has been attained spontaneously, but Zen meditation offers a systematic way to cultivate the direct experience of transcending space and time.

At the time U.S. astronauts first walked on the moon, Charles and I were living on the Navajo reservation. There was extensive news coverage of the moon walk on TV and in the newspapers. One old Navajo man said to me, "I don't know what all the fuss is about. Navajo medicine men have been walking on the moon for hundreds of years." His comment and the way he said it stayed with me for a long time and I wondered how the medicine men did it. Many years later, in the direct experience of emptiness, I saw that there is no distance between me and the moon. There is no distance whatsoever between me and the mountains, rivers, trees, birds, and all the people of the earth. In our essential nature we are one. When I saw this, the thought came through my mind, "Oh, now I know how the medicine man walked on the moon."

One hot summer evening, we were meditating in Roshi Kennedy's meditation room in the Jesuit dormitory at St. Peter's College in Jersey City. Through the open window we could hear all the sounds of the city: beeping horns, sirens, car alarms, and people milling around in the streets talking. We sat round after round and at the end of each round Roshi Kennedy lit another stick of incense and we continued sitting into the night. The atmosphere in the room was subtle and refined and I remember thinking, "There is nowhere else on earth I'd rather be than right here. I've waited millions of years for this." When the last period of meditation ended, Roshi Kennedy went over to the window and gazed up at the full moon and said, "Take a good look at the moon. It will never be fuller or closer than it is tonight."

You don't have to do Zen meditation only in a meditation room. You can sit out under the stars. Any place you sit is one with the whole universe. Every place you sit or stand or walk is a holy place. Each day when I enter the hospital to go to work, I think to myself, "Enter this great house with a prayer. This is a sacred place. People are being born, healed, and dying here today." As caregivers we create a healing environment—a space conducive to healing. At the same time we transcend space because healing takes place right where you are.

# RIGHT NOW:

## *Transcending Time*

Life is lived right now in the present moment. In the past and in the future life is only a thought. It is not life itself. Likewise, healing takes place right now in the present moment. You can only experience wholeness and the fullness of life right here and now. This very moment is the only moment you have.

One day I drove off to do some errands and before I went a block, I saw a man lying in the road seriously injured. A car had run into him and thrown him down onto the pavement. There was only one passerby at the scene, so he went off to call 911 and I stayed with the injured man. I quickly checked him over, helped him stay still, and had him take some slow breaths. I reassured him and told him that help was on the way. We were together for a few minutes until the rescue squad arrived. In those few moments we were fully present and we knew each other. I was sad to hear that he died a few days later and although I knew him for only those few moments, I miss him and feel the loss of his death.

In our culture we are time-bound and tend to run around at a frantic and hectic pace. Sometimes when we are ill, life comes to an abrupt standstill. We have to call work and explain that we are sick and will be taking some time off until we feel better. When we are admitted to the hospital, time stops and our usual routine is suspended for a while. Meditation is an opportunity to slow down for twenty-five minutes, to stop for a moment and take time to heal.

When Charles and I lived on the Navajo reservation, there were many jokes about Navajo time. The Navajo people were not time-bound. They did each thing in its time. Now we are living in southwestern Virginia where people move and speak more slowly than they do where we grew up in the Finger Lakes region of New York State. We sometimes joke that things move so slowly down here in Virginia that it takes an hour to do a twenty-five-minute meditation. One busy day at work, I was running up and down the hall at the hospital tending to several patients at the same time and an elderly gentleman sitting in a gerichair said to me, "Slow down. You'll strip a gear." During meditation you slow down, sit still, and let your mind settle. It is a good antidote to our overly busy lives.

Once Roshi Glassman began a Zen talk saying, "Once upon a time in a galaxy far, far away. When is once upon a time? Right now! Where is far, far away? Right here!" In good Zen form, he shouted "Right now!" and "Right here!" so forcefully it shook the rafters and jolted me into the present. Zen takes place in the present moment. Life takes place in the present moment. As the Zen saying goes, "Eternity is nothing other than right now."

Individual meetings with the Zen teacher are brief encounters. There is a sense of immediacy, openness, and spontaneity. It is not a fifty-minute counseling session. It is not a philosophical, theological, or theoretical discussion. It is a presentation of self and how you are seeing things in the present moment to which the Zen teacher spontaneously responds. Then the student responds without a moment's hesitation. It is a vital meeting, a sharing, a pointing, an experiencing, and an expressing that occurs in just a few moments.

One day a monk went to meet with Zen Master Jo and asked him, "Daitsu Chisho Buddha sat in the meditation hall for ten *kalpas*, but the dharma of the Buddha did not manifest itself and he could not attain Buddhahood. Why was this?" Jo replied, "Because he is a nonattained Buddha." A *kalpa* is an infinitely long period of time. This koan is pushing you to transcend time. It doesn't matter how long Daitsu Chisho Buddha sat in the meditation hall; he could not attain Buddhahood, or his essential nature, because he was already Buddha. Experiencing your essential nature is not a matter of putting in time. It is not a matter of becoming someone or something else. In this story, the monk is like a person who asks a child, "What do you want to be when you grow up?" He is imposing the idea of time and development on a life and missing the fact that the child is already complete and whole just as he is right now. Experiencing your essential nature is a matter of opening your eyes and seeing what already is right now. It is the ongoing process of seeing your essential nature from moment to moment.

Once Zen Master Baso was seriously ill. The chief priest of the temple came to visit him and asked, "How do you feel these days?" Baso replied, "Sun-faced Buddha, Moon-faced Buddha."

Buddhist sutras tell us Sun-faced Buddha lived for eighteen hundred years and Moon-faced Buddha lived for only one day and one night. What does Baso tell us about his experience of illness by saying, "Sun-faced Buddha, Moon-faced Buddha?" With his cryptic response, Baso suggests that he is fully experiencing the present moment. He is fully present in each moment and will continue to be fully present in each moment whether he lives for many years or for only one day and a night. He is experiencing and savoring each moment whether it is the warmth of the sun or the cool glow of the moon. Each moment is whole and he is present. Right now, this very moment, Baso is whole and healed even in the midst of serious illness.

Kari, a little girl with leukemia who I took care of, had a wish. Her wish was that she would go into remission again and that she would get to go home and invite all of her family and friends over for a picnic out on the lawn. She would sit on the grass with her cousins and friends and they all would eat fried chicken. But she did not go into remission. Instead she took a sudden turn for the worse one evening and died. I took care of her during the day shift on the day she died. As I was leaving for home, I stopped by her room to say, "Good-bye. I'll see you tomorrow." Kari looked up at me and she said, "I think we better have that picnic now."

Kari reminds us that transcending time is the ending of time. Tomorrow is only an idea. The truth of the matter is that this moment, like the breath, is the only one you have. And like the breath, you need to allow each moment to nourish and sustain you. When the idea of time is transcended, you will find yourself living in the timeless present that is whole and complete.

# FRESHNESS:
## *Always New*

Each morning welcomes in a new day, fresh and full of possibilities. If you are completely open, not holding on to any thoughts, opinions, or images, something new can be seen. A new sun rises. You really wake up and experience life fully for the first time.

Sometimes the experience of having a serious illness and facing death wakes a person up to what is most meaningful in life. The person facing death begins to cherish each day and live each moment fully. But you don't need to wait until you are seriously ill to learn this lesson. You can be born this moment to new ways of seeing and being in the world. You can choose to wake up and see each moment fresh and new and live each day with vitality and appreciation.

In my work as a nursing professor, I get to view the health care system through new eyes each semester. Each semester brings a new group of nursing students experiencing the clinical setting for the first time. They notice the care patients receive and they raise questions if they observe any incompetence or insensitivity. They are idealistic and caring and I try to keep them that way.

Often nursing students are particularly moved when they first watch the birth of a baby and the first time a patient they are caring for dies. One student described with tears in her eyes her first time being in the delivery room for the birth of a baby. She said that when the baby was first born he opened his eyes and looked around the room to see where he had arrived. She couldn't believe how alert the baby was and how tiny his little hands and feet were. The miracle of birth was thoroughly amazing to her and she was extremely grateful that she got to be in the delivery room and share the experience.

Every day of life is amazing if we view it through fresh eyes. We are being born each moment. If we are present to experience the miracle of each moment we are extremely grateful for the experience of being alive.

One student movingly described her first time caring for a patient who died. The patient was a man in his sixties who had suffered several strokes and was now unconscious. The student spent the day helping the nurse care for the man while the doctors and the family made the decision to discontinue the life support equipment and allow the man to die. The student agreed with the doctors and family that it was the best thing to do, but still it felt so sad, so silent, and so final. The student said she cried and prayed with the family as the tubes and wires were disconnected from the man and he breathed his last breaths. Afterwards, the family left and the student helped the nurse clean the patient one last time and prepare him for transport. She said it was the first time she had ever touched a dead person and she could feel that the life had left his body. She was filled with many emotions, with many questions about life and death, and with the sensation of death, which she had never felt before. Death felt vast and quiet and still. She said her first experience of death gave her a deeper appreciation for life. When she walked out of the hospital at the end of the day, she couldn't believe how green the grass and trees were, how blue the sky was, and how fresh the breeze felt blowing across her cheeks.

Many years ago in China, a monk named Hui-ming followed Zen Master Hui-neng up into the mountains and sought instruction from him. Hui-neng said to the monk, "Not thinking of good, not thinking of evil, at this very moment, what is your original face?" This is similar to the well-known Zen koan, "Show me your face before your parents were born."

Hui-neng was urging Hui-ming to go beyond dualistic thoughts such as good and evil, subject and object, success and failure. Transcending dualistic thought, Hui-ming directly experienced his essential nature or his original face. The koan, "Show me your face before your parents were born" moves you to transcend space and time and experience your essential nature or original face right here and now. With the direct experience of transcending thought, space, and time, comes a great awakening. You wake up and feel the warmth of the sun on your original face. With this experience you see things in a new way and begin living life with freshness and vitality this very moment.

Life lived fresh and new is rich and vibrant. It is like fresh vegetables picked in the garden and eaten the same day. Sometimes produce from the grocery store is lack-luster. It was picked long ago, transported from far away, and stored on the shelf for days. It is limp and lacking in flavor. Leaf lettuce eaten straight from the garden is crisp, bright green, fresh, and flavorful. It's like eating a sunny summer day.

Zen practice helps you live each day as if it were your first day on earth. You learn to live with the sensitivity and wonder of a newborn baby, bright-eyed, seeing everything for the first time. We walk on this earth with the excitement of a toddler taking her first steps, thrilled to be standing on her own two feet and moving through space.

When my daughter was first learning to walk, she would pull herself up and take two or three steps. A big smile would spread across her face as she moved across the room. Then, *plop*, she would fall down onto her bottom. When she fell down she did not consider herself a failure or spend time worrying about making a mistake. She didn't get bogged down in dualistic thought like good and bad or success and failure. Without hesitation, she got right back up and took two or three more steps before plopping down onto her bottom again. She re-peated this over and over again, delighting in the whole process.

As an adult you do not have to lose the delight in life that a young child experiences. As you grow older you gain knowledge, life experience, and maturity, but you do not have to let them bind you. Zen practice helps you transcend the boundaries of knowledge, life experience, and maturity. You become flexible and able to both know and not know. You learn from life experience and also learn to experience things freshly, in the present moment, as if for the first time. You become mature, but not rigid. You regain your original sense of wonder and freshness.

Each Monday morning, my mother goes out to her quilting group in Floyd, Virginia. She gathers her fabrics, scissors, spools of thread, needles, and thimble into a basket and drives off into the hills. Every week she learns new ways to stitch pieces of fabric together to create something beautiful. Each of her quilts is a unique transformation of the old into the new. The quilts are cherished and handed down from generation to generation. Each generation experiences anew the warmth, color, texture, and beauty of the quilts.

When my father was in the hospital, my mother brought him the bow-tie quilt she made. She chose a bow-tie pattern because for many years he wore a bow-tie to work every day. The bow-ties and borders were in soft greens and browns because these were his favorite colors. The browns were like fresh plowed earth and the greens like the thousand shades of green of new leaves on the trees in early spring. I watched as my mother carefully placed the quilt over my father resting in bed. The soft earth colors had a healing effect in the cold, impersonal hospital room. The quilt brought warmth and comfort to my father and I was happy to see a renewed freshness in his eyes, face, and spirit.

There are many ways to bring freshness and healing into your life and the life of the person you are caring for. Bringing plants, flowers, and fresh fruit into your room or the room of the person who is ill can awaken the senses and reconnect you with things that are fresh and growing. Music, artwork, photographs, fresh sheets and pillowcases, soft pajamas and slippers, and freshly cooked food from home can all have a healing effect. Also a simple smile is always fresh and new and brings healing to both the person who smiles and the person who sees the smile.

# APPRECIATION:

## *Saying Thank You*

To appreciate is to really see or really hear, and having really seen or heard, to say, "Wow! Isn't this incredible! Isn't this wonderful!" Appreciation is the soft sigh of a heartfelt, "Thank you." Appreciation is thinking, "I'm grateful for this experience." Appreciation is feeling, "I'm glad to be alive and to have the opportunity to walk on this earth." This is very different from the feelings of depression and despair so many people all around us are having these days. Some people feel entitlement and disappointment rather than appreciation. An attitude of appreciation is healing.

My great-great-great-aunt, Anna Howard Shaw, took care of Susan B. Anthony at the time of her death. In Anna's biography, she tells a very moving story about gratitude and the expression of appreciation:

> During the last forty-eight hours of her life she was unwilling that I should leave her side. So day and night I knelt by her bed, holding her hand and watching the wonderful flame of her spirit grow dim. At times, even then, it blazed up with startling suddenness. On the last afternoon of her life, when she had lain quiet for hours, she suddenly began to utter the names of the women who had worked with her, as if in a final roll call. Many of them had preceded her

into the next world; others were still splendidly active in the work she was laying down. But young or old, living or dead, they all seemed to file past her dying eyes that day in an endless, shadowy review, and as they went by she spoke to each of them. Not all the names she mentioned were known in suffrage ranks; some of these women lived only in the heart of Susan B. Anthony, and now, for the last time, she was thanking them.

Being grateful and expressing appreciation are unifying and healing. They enable people to work together for the good of each other and of the earth.

In college most of us were required to take a course in music appreciation or art appreciation. The goal of these courses was to expose us to great music or works of art and to guide us in developing an appreciation for the richness, beauty, and human qualities expressed in them.

This brings to mind my Zen teacher, Roshi Kennedy, who often listens to Puccini before going off to work for the day. After singing along with some heart-wrenching aria, he goes off inspired, energized, and humanized. One morning when Charles and I were visiting him, he played the soundtrack to *Romeo and Juliet* at high volume while he shaved and got dressed. Just before gathering his papers and heading out the door, he paused for a moment listening to the theme song and said to Charles and me, "Fill your minds with this!" When times are difficult, it is healing to surround yourself with beauty—music that inspires you, art that moves you, and people who love you.

Zen Master Seppo once said, "All the great world, if I pick it up with my fingertips, is found to be like a grain of rice. I throw it in front of your face, but you do not see it. Beat the drum, telling the monks to come out to work, and search for it." Imagine the awe and wonder of seeing the entire universe in each grain of rice. Sitting in the silence of meditation you naturally develop this kind of profound appreciation. When you take the time to truly see, hear, and appreciate everything around you, each thing can inspire you, energize you, and enrich your life.

A middle-aged man I know injured his back at work and had to spend several months recuperating at home. He was home alone all day while his wife was away at work and as he rested there in the quiet house, he began noticing the birds moving around outside his window, breaking the silence with their calls. He and his wife began putting bird seed out in feeders for them and he found himself spending more time each day watching them. His special friend was a woodpecker who drummed on the gutter pipe from time to time. During his time of healing, he developed an appreciation for all the different kinds of birds that came into his yard and he began to recognize each species by its song. Before his back injury he never paid much attention to birds, but now he appreciated their beauty and variety and he was thankful for their company during his long recovery.

Often in the evening at a Zen retreat, the four vows are chanted. One of the vows is, "Dharmas are boundless. I vow to perceive them." The word "dharma" means the teaching or truth. Each person, each plant, each animal, and each rock has its own unique reality, truth, or beauty. Each person, plant, animal, and rock has something to teach us if we take the time to really look and listen. In the chanting of this vow is the intention to appreciate the reality, truth, and beauty of everything in the universe. This vow keeps you curious and intensely interested in the flow of life within and all around you each moment.

During the summer Pat brings us fresh green beans from her garden when she comes to meditate on Monday evenings. Can we fully appreciate the green color, crisp texture, and fresh flavor of each tender new bean? One Saturday morning I bought a peck of fresh peaches from a local farmer. The peach fragrance filled the kitchen. They were tree-ripened, rich-colored, sweet, and juicy. Biting into one of them, the juice ran down my chin and wrist and splashed on the kitchen floor. I fully appreciated each flavorful bite.

Charles planted pumpkins again this year. Each day he goes out to water them and invites me to come out and admire them. They are especially beautiful in the misty morning when the large school-bus-colored blossoms reach up to the sky like stars. The neighbor boys are duly impressed with the long vines growing out across the lawn and up the pine trees. One little boy was amazed to hear that the pumpkins grew from pumpkin seeds scraped out of last year's pumpkins. There is a Zen koan that asks,

"What is Buddha?" Answers abound—a green bean, a ripe peach, a pumpkin blossom. We can find Buddha everywhere.

I grew up in western New York near the Seneca village Ganondagan. The Senecas believe that it is the duty of human beings to enhance the life force of the earth through celebration, consciousness, and responsible behavior. This belief was the source of their ceremonial year following the cycles of nature. For me, Zen practice is a way to increase awareness and appreciation of nature and to nurture responsible behavior toward the earth. Silent sitting in meditation is an expression of gratitude for the opportunity to be a human being living on this earth for a short while. A life lived with great appreciation is a great life.

Often I encourage my nursing students to really appreciate and value each person they take care of. I tell them that a good way to do this is to care for each person as if they were your own mother, father, sister, brother, or child. When you appreciate how much a person means to those who love him or her, you are motivated to do all you can to provide comfort and promote healing. One student took care of an eighteen-year-old boy for two days after his surgery. Each morning she shampooed his hair and helped him fix it the way he liked it. When she was getting ready to leave the second day, he thanked her for all she had done for him, but most of all for helping him with his hair. She told me she knew how much time her younger brother spent in front of the mirror fixing his hair and that's what he would want help with the most if he were in the hospital.

Many nurses tell me that the high point of their career is when a patient says, "Thank you. You really helped me." For the nurse, knowing that she has helped, renews her spirit and gives her the energy to keep going. The expression of gratitude is healing for both the giver and the receiver.

# III

# COMPASSIONATE ACTION: REACHING OUT WITH HEALING HANDS

# TOUCHING:
## *The Touch That Heals*

Touch is a very basic human need. Infants die if they are not held and touched. Our need for touch extends across the life span. As a nurse I touch patients throughout the day as I provide physical care. The way I touch a patient can communicate that I am in a hurry and that the patient is simply someone next on the list. Or my touch can communicate caring and human-to-human contact. My hands can convey love and compassion.

Paul, an elderly man I took care of, lived alone and had many physical problems. One day he returned from his physical therapy appointment and told me that the therapist had massaged and applied heat to his back and legs with such care. He hadn't felt so good in years. He said, "I felt cherished." In addition to feeling good physically Paul felt valued and cared for. He felt a human-to-human connection.

Touch is not a thought. It is a direct experience. Infants and children learn by touching. They reach out to touch and handle whatever they see. Infants don't just touch with their little hands, but also with their mouths. With delight a baby discovers his toe and promptly sticks it into his mouth and sucks on it for a while. A young child in an antique shop feels the need to reach for everything in sight. The child's natural tendency is to touch and to learn. As an adult you can continue to learn and grow by touching the world around you and letting yourself be touched by it.

A ninety-two-year-old man I took care of named Carl fell and broke his arm while climbing on a ladder to clean leaves out of the gutters of his house. His daughter told him over and over again not to do jobs like that by himself anymore. She tried to get him to wait until the evening or weekend when she or her brother could do jobs that required climbing on ladders or stepping stools. But he had always been very independent and didn't listen to her. Over time his walking became progressively more unsteady, but whenever she tried to take his hand to steady him he pulled away. One day when she took his hand and he pulled away she said, "You know Dad, this isn't about helping you so you don't fall. This is about holding hands. I want to hold your hand." From that day on he never pulled away again and they hold hands often when they are walking.

One day in ancient times sixteen bodhisattvas went to take their baths and with the touch of the warm water, they suddenly experienced realization. They exclaimed, "We experienced the subtle and clear touch, have attained Buddhahood, and still retain it." The touch of the warm bath water on the skin of the bodhisattvas was the trigger for their awakening. For some people the sense of sight, such as seeing the morning star or seeing the peach blossoms, was the catalyst for an awakening experience. For others the catalyst was the sense of sound, such as the sound of a pebble hitting bamboo or the ringing of a temple bell. Touching, seeing, and hearing are all direct experiences in the present moment. In direct experience, thoughts and concepts are transcended and essential nature can be experienced.

Once during a break at a Zen retreat a woman went out for a walk in the woods behind the Zen center. After a while she stopped along the path to take a little rest. She leaned her back against a huge old pine tree and with a sigh she released the tension she felt in her belly. Suddenly she could see clearly that she was not separate from the rough bark of the tree, the pine needles beneath her feet, or the vast sky. She was everything she saw and she laughed and cried at the sheer beauty of it.

When an awakening experience occurs, you begin Zen practice anew. It is not an endpoint or a goal that has been reached. In order to retain the vitality and freshness of the realization, you keep going, touching life moment by moment. The experience cannot be grasped or held on to. There is a Zen saying, "Seeking it oneself with empty hands, you return with empty hands." Empty hands are open hands reaching out to others and to the unknown.

In the Buddhist tradition, the bodhisattva of compassion is Kannon. She is sometimes portrayed as having a thousand hands. Each hand responds in a particular way to heal suffering in the world. One hand allays fear, one fights for justice, and one heals disease. Having gained realization the bodhisattva reaches out to heal the world of suffering.

The most famous Zen koan is "What is the sound of one hand clapping?" This koan points you toward the direct experience of one hand. The hand that holds is one with the hand that is held. Although the right hand and the left hand are different from each other, they are of one body. Although my hand and your hand are different from each other, they are of one body. When I hold a patient's hand to reassure and provide comfort, it is the one hand.

One night I was assigned to provide one-to-one care for a little boy in the pediatric intensive care unit. He had been shot in a hunting accident and was critically wounded. He was on a respirator and lay there unconscious. His mother sat by his bedside all night holding his hand and saying repeatedly, "I'm here with you." His mother thanked me for taking such excellent care of her son and said she felt so helpless. I told her that her reassuring voice and the feel of her hand in his was what her son really needed from her right now.

The well-known series of ten Zen ox-herding pictures depict ever-deepening levels of spiritual development. In the first picture, a person sets out in search of the ox that symbolizes one's essential nature. The person subsequently glimpses, catches, tames, and rides the ox and deeply experiences essential nature, or oneness. However, this is not the end of the journey. The tenth picture is titled "Entering the Marketplace with Helping Hands." The verse that accompanies the final picture is:

*Barechested, barefooted, he comes into the marketplace.*
*Muddied and dust-covered, how broadly he grins!*
*Without recourse to mystic powers,*
*Withered trees he swiftly brings to bloom.*

After realizing his essential nature, he looks like an ordinary person and he enters fully into the activities of the everyday world living among ordinary people. He does not possess any mystical powers, but he is whole and free. His smile radiates peace and inspires those around him to be healed and to blossom. He returns with helping hands, reaching out to touch and heal the world around him.

# CLEANING:
## *Making Life Sparkle*

One of the first patients I took care of when I was a nursing student was a man who was found passed out in the street after a drinking binge. He was semicomatose, had liver damage, was homeless, and hadn't taken a bath in a very long time. All I had learned so far in my first semester of nursing school was checking vital signs, making beds, and giving bedbaths. It took me all morning to get the man cleaned up, check his vital signs, and change his bed. I remember feeling proud as I left the unit at noon with him clean as a whistle resting comfortably between crisp white sheets. Mundane tasks like cleaning are an essential aspect of healing.

I was moved when I read in the journals of Abraham Maslow about his impressions of the nursing students who helped take care of him in the hospital after he had a heart attack. He said that after spending most of his life as a university professor, he had never encountered a group of students as altruistic as the nursing students. He was amazed that they were even pleased when he was able to move his bowels and they cheerfully emptied the bedpan. The nursing students viewed meeting basic human needs, like the need to go to the bathroom and to clean up afterward, as an important part of caring for the whole person.

Maslow thought they could serve as role models of self-actualized behavior for the rest of our society.

Barbara, a home health nurse, once told me that some of the most intimate moments in her interactions with her elderly homebound patients occur while providing foot care. While she soaks and washes the patients' feet and trims their nails, often they speak with her about some of their greatest joys or deepest concerns. As a Christian, the scene from the Bible where Jesus washed the disciples' feet comes to her mind at these times. The patients say that foot care is what they need most since they are no longer able to do it for themselves. In these moments of physically caring for the patient's feet, Barbara and her patients talk with each other and experience a real feeling of connection.

When entering a Zen meditation hall, you are impressed by the cleanliness and orderliness of the room. The floor is clean and the mats and cushions are arranged in neat rows. Cleanliness and order contribute to the aesthetics of Zen. There is a sense of simplicity and clarity. A clean uncluttered environment creates visual silence and spaciousness in which the mind can settle and be calm, expanding into the present moment.

In some ways a Zen hall is like a Montessori classroom. A Montessori classroom is very orderly and at the same time rich with materials and equipment for the children to handle and learn from. Low shelves line the walls so the children can easily select what they want to work with and can return each thing to its place when they are finished. Throughout the day the children participate in washing their hands, washing tables, and cleaning up after activities. It is an environment and routine that is carefully designed to promote the growth and development of young children.

A Zen hall is an environment that is designed to help adults take another step in their growth and development. Within the hall both beauty and discipline are integrated to encourage the mind to move beyond its habitual ways of thinking and perceiving and to experience something new. The meditators arrive five minutes before the sitting period begins and they do not bring any extra clutter into the room with them. Shoes are left outside the meditation hall on shelves or lined up against the wall. Silence is maintained in the hall and the meditators sit as still as possible so they don't distract others. The beauty of the Zen hall is the simplicity, the flowers on the table, and the sound of the bell signaling the beginning and end of sitting. In this orderly environment the mind is freed to fully experience the present moment. Many people create an uncluttered, aesthetically pleasing space in their homes for daily meditation.

During work periods in a Zen monastery, monks can be seen mopping floors, cleaning bathrooms, sweeping sidewalks, pulling weeds, and raking leaves. The kitchen is kept immaculately clean and food is meticulously prepared to nourish the community. Cleanliness is valued. The theme of cleaning is encountered repeatedly in the Zen koans.

A well-known example is the koan about a poetry contest. Zen Master Hung-jen was the abbot of a great Zen monastery in China. When he grew old and it became time for him to select a successor to carry on the teaching, he announced that there would be a poetry contest. He would hand on his teaching to the monk who wrote a verse that demonstrated the greatest degree of realization. The head monk Shen-hsiu composed the following verse:

> *The body is the tree of enlightenment;*
> *The mind is like a bright mirror-stand.*
> *Wipe it clean over and over,*
> *And do not let the dust gather.*

Zen Master Hung-jen praised the verse publicly and all the monks thought Shen-hsiu would become the next abbot. However an illiterate monk, named Hui-neng, who worked in the rice-hulling shed, composed the following verse in response to Shen-hsiu's verse:

> *Enlightenment is essentially not a tree;*
> *The bright mirror is not a stand.*
> *From the beginning, not a single thing exists;*
> *Where can the dust collect?*

Zen Master Hung-jen handed on his robe and his bowl to Hui-neng who went on to become the famous Sixth Patriarch of China.

The first verse describes the process of sitting up straight in meditation and allowing the mind to settle. In this calm state, the mind is freed from its habitual nonstop thought patterns and you can see the nature of mind and the world around you more clearly. Shen-hsiu says that you have to wipe your perception clean over and over again. He is emphasizing the need to sit in meditation every morning and evening day after day. Our habits of thought are deeply ingrained and the clarity we experience through meditation is quickly obscured without ongoing attention and practice.

While Shen-hsui's verse communicates a valuable insight, Hui-neng's verse is even more subtle and profound. His verse gives you a glimpse into the essential nature of yourself and the universe. From the point of view of essential nature, there is no need for cleaning. No static things exist for dirt to cling to. The essential nature of every person and every thing is already clean and pure. Of course, there is the need to wake up and realize this and to live your life accordingly.

Several years ago Roshi Brantchen, a Zen teacher from Switzerland, invited my husband and me to attend an interreligious conference he was sponsoring about peace, justice, and the integrity of the earth. After the conference he drove us across Switzerland to his home village of Ronda, high in the Swiss Alps near the Matterhorn. Switzerland is an incredibly beautiful country with so many lakes, mountains, and meadows but what impressed me the most was that whether in the cities or in the country there was no litter along the roadsides. When I returned home to the United States, the copious amounts of litter along our streets and roads saddened me. What kind of mind and attitude allows people to trash their own country? I had seen that unlittered highways are a possibility and I could see that the beautiful mountains, lakes, and rivers surrounding my home in southwest Virginia would be as beautiful as Switzerland without the all-pervasive litter. There is a need to wake up, to see the beauty that surrounds us, and to demonstrate respect for the earth by keeping our own country clean. Disrespect for the earth and a littered environment wound the spirit. Respect for the earth and the beauty of nature heal and enliven the spirit.

Zen Master Ju-ching cleaned the monastery toilets even after he became abbot. He cleaned the toilets as a sign of his gratitude for the teaching he had received, in response to the simple reality that toilets need to be cleaned, and because he realized that cleaning toilets is the functioning of essential nature. Essential nature can be directly experienced in even the most mundane or distasteful aspects of life. In the experience of nonduality you move beyond the discriminating, judging mind that labels activities as mundane or exciting, pleasant or distasteful, high status or low status. Ju-ching was not limited by viewing his work cleaning toilets as lowly or demeaning. He was a shining role model for us in seeing that all of the work that needs to be done is to be embraced as a facet of the whole of life.

The families of patients I took care of while they were dying often expressed to me much gratitude for keeping their dying family member clean and comfortable. Often patients became so ill and weak that they were incontinent. Keeping the patient comfortably positioned in a clean bed, dressed in clean pajamas with a blue pad beneath them, and cleaning them up as soon as they went to the bathroom were essential tasks of caring for a dying person. Going to the bathroom and cleaning up afterward are aspects of the whole of life. This too is our essential nature and the essential nature of the universe. While volumes have been written in recent years about the psychological and spiritual care of the dying, inadequate attention has been given to the importance of providing good basic physical care. Many dying people do not receive adequate physical care. This aspect of care is very demanding and family caregivers often become exhausted and run down even to the point of becoming physically ill from having to do it all by themselves. Reaching out to provide physical assistance such as cleaning, bathing, and doing laundry is a great act of compassion. Cleaning is an important aspect of the art of healing.

# WORKING:

## *Making a Contribution*

Through your work you make a contribution to your family and to your community. Your work is an important aspect of who you are as a whole person. To be able to find meaningful work and to be able to hold down a job are signs of good mental health. To be willing to work is a sign of good character. Often when people are seriously ill they long to recover and return to their normal routine of family and work life. If you do your work with integrity and attention it is healing both to yourself and the people around you.

A person is not separate from his or her family, community, culture, or work. One time when I led a workshop on "Spirituality and Healing," a physician in the group came up to me afterward and described his experience being a patient recovering from coronary bypass surgery. He said he wanted so badly to recover so he could return to work. His father had been a physician before him and he was carrying on his father's calling. For him being a doctor was not just a matter of physical healing, but also included spiritual healing and presence, although he had never felt free to talk openly about this aspect of his practice lest he be viewed as less than scientific by the medical community. He said his work healed himself as well as others.

Work is valued in the Zen tradition. Zen is not a matter of being versus doing. Being and doing are not separate. You need to be able to do both. The awareness and presence you practice in meditation are carried into your daily life and work. You are present in your work in body, mind, and spirit.

Zen meditation is itself a form of work, not just a relaxation technique. You work during meditation to stay awake, pay attention, and move beyond delusions and daydreams. You don't just sit there thinking in your usual way. "Just sitting" is not just sitting. You work to let go of your habitual patterns of thought and open to something new.

Often manual labor has been associated with low socioeconomic status or low rank. However, in the Zen monastery everyone is expected to do manual labor. In Zen monasteries one of the highest ranked positions is the cook. This is an ingenious, pragmatic approach that ensures that the community will be well nourished and enjoy the wonderful tastes of the food available to them. Hui-neng, one of the most well known and highly esteemed of the ancient Chinese Zen masters, worked in the rice-hulling shed. Another great Chinese Zen master, Luohen Guichen, was often seen raking the monastery grounds or mopping the floor of the Zen hall.

Once a Trappist monk attending a Zen retreat I was at gave a talk about contemplative life in the Catholic tradition. He said that prior to entering the monastery, he read many books describing the mystical experiences of contemplatives down through the ages. It was all so interesting and exciting. However, he said his experience of the contemplative life was silently planting rhubarb. First he dug a hole. Then he worked manure into the soil with his hands. Then he put in the rhubarb and patted it into place.

One nurse I know is the nurse manager of a busy medical-surgical unit at a local hospital. Several times a month she works a shift as a staff nurse. She says it keeps up her clinical skills and gives her the opportunity for patient contact that is meaningful to her. Working alongside the staff nurses also demonstrates to them that she knows firsthand the difficulties and the value of the work they do. This greatly contributes to morale on the unit.

When you are recovering from an illness or coping with a chronic one, completing some simple chores can help you regain or maintain your strength, flexibility, and stamina. The gentle movements involved in doing the dishes, watering the plants, and folding the clothes when they come out of the dryer, connect you with the rhythm of daily life. Often people feel better about themselves when they are able not only to be helped by others, but also to help others in some way. Reading to the children, helping them with their homework, and writing letters are ways to help that aren't physically demanding.

To value work is a very practical matter. Zen Master Pai-chang said that a day without work is a day without eating. We work to meet our basic human needs for food, clothing, and shelter. We work to help those who are unable to meet their needs.

At a Zen retreat, in addition to extended periods of meditation, the daily schedule includes a work period. This is called work practice. While doing your assigned job, the silence of the retreat is maintained. The mind is alert while doing the task and not thinking about other things or daydreaming. Manual labor moves you out of the head and into the body. Without preoccupation you are one with the work.

I can clearly remember the work I was assigned to do during work periods at the first Zen retreat I attended. My job was to carry large rocks up a dusty mountainside to build a retaining wall. A monk who lived at the Zen center silently guided the project, showing us where to place the rocks. At the time it struck me as very Zenlike work, moving a mountain rock by rock to keep the mountain from moving. At many retreats since that time, I have washed windows, cleaned bathrooms, weeded gardens, picked fruit, stuffed envelopes, prepared food, washed dishes, pulled nails from old boards, and swept out an old barn. Successfully completing a variety of jobs engenders self-confidence and a sense of the dignity of work.

Once Zen Master Basiasita asked one of his students, "What thing will you not do?" The student answered, "I will not do any ordinary thing." Basiasita then asked, "What thing must you do?" The student answered, "I must do Buddha work."

"Buddha work" means to clarify and awaken to your essential nature which is the essential nature of the universe. Having done that, no work you do is ordinary. All work is Buddha work.

One of the steps of Buddha's Eightfold Path is Right Livelihood. Right Livelihood means choosing a job or career that enhances the life of others and of the earth. It means not choosing one that harms other people or destroys the earth, which supports the life of plants, animals, and people. This is a complex consideration and is often not clear-cut, but in general this is an important guiding principle. The work you do should not just be a way to make money. It should make a worthwhile contribution to the well-being of people and of the planet. In addition, Right Livelihood applies to how you do the work you do and to working toward more humanistic and ecological methods and working conditions.

I selected nursing as a profession, after a month-long period of intensive meditation during summer vacation from my job as a first grade teacher. I had gotten to know several excellent public health nurses while I was living out on the Navajo reservation. These nurses worked closely with the people in the clinic, in the schools, and in the hogans. They were very knowledgeable and worked independently since the nearest hospital was forty miles away and the doctor only came out to the town once a week. The people often turned to these nurses in times of emergency and in appreciation included them in their Navajo celebrations. I knew I wanted to work closely with people and I could see that as a nurse I would be able to serve and support people in their birthing, living, and dying.

It is sad to me that some of the best nurses I have known are no longer working as nurses. Donna, a nurse I knew when I worked in the neonatal intensive care unit, was bright, energetic, capable, very caring toward the babies and their parents, and able to start an IV in a premature infant when all the visible veins were used up. Donna is the nurse I would choose to take care of my own baby. But she is now a real estate agent. Many nurses find jobs in other fields because of short staffing and poor working conditions in hospitals and health care agencies. Sometimes the work that most needs to be done is working to improve working conditions. Improving working conditions is one way to care for caregivers so they can work to heal others.

Work can be a spiritual practice, just as sitting meditation and walking meditation are spiritual practices. During meditation I am aware of my own breath. At work in the hospital I watch another's breath. During walking meditation I am aware of my walking. At work I help an old man walk the length of the hall. When starting an IV my attention is on gathering the supplies, spotting a vein, cleaning the site, inserting the needle, threading the catheter, and neatly taping it in place. Simultaneously, I am aware of the human being I am interacting with, conversing with, and touching in a caring manner. Attending to each task and each person, I am one with my work and everything around me.

# SEEING:

## Responding to What You See

Healing requires a shift in perception so your vision is expanded and you see your wholeness. Often people develop tunnel vision and they do not see the many options and alternatives that are open to them. Or they do not see their situation for what it is, but rather remain in denial. We need to be encouraged to see things afresh, with honesty and awareness. Healing occurs when our eyes are opened and our vision is expanded and clarified.

Zen practice is a way to clarify and expand your vision. For example, when you sit in Zen meditation your eyes are open. You are awake and alert to what is right in front of you. You do not close your eyes to what is difficult or unpleasant. And you don't just see with your eyes. Zen practice teaches you to see with your whole body and mind.

When you go in to see a Zen teacher for an individual meeting, there is usually a flower in a vase on the table. Sometimes the Zen teacher wants to know if you can see the flower. Can you really see the flower? The Zen teacher wants you to demonstrate what you are seeing and experiencing in meditation and in life. Don't discuss or explain. Present yourself and what you see directly. Most people can see and appreciate the beautiful color and form of a flower. But the Zen teacher wants you to also see right through to the essential nature of the flower. There is a Zen saying, "Seeing, hearing, forms, and sounds, are nothing else than Mind." In really seeing the flower, you experience that you and the flower are Big Mind or essential nature. It is Big Mind or essential nature that sees.

This way of seeing is helpful to me when I am taking care of a person who is ill and suffering. I see the details of the person's condition—his color, respiratory effort, facial expression, and position. Based on my careful observations, I intervene to improve the person's condition or to help him feel more comfortable. At the same time, I am able to see the whole person who is there before me and I am able to remain in touch with the energy and unity of all creation. Healing requires clarity and vision that is both sharp and broad.

There is a koan called "Joshu Sees Through an Old Woman" in which an old woman ran a teahouse by the side of the road on the way to Mount Taizan. Frequently a monk would stop by on the way to study Zen at the monastery up on Mount Taizan. The monk would have something to eat and drink and then ask the old woman for directions. Each time she responded the same way telling him "Go straight on." After the monk proceeded a few steps, but was still within earshot, she commented, "This good, honest monk goes off that way too." The monks on Mount Taizan were frustrated and perplexed by this so they asked Zen Master Joshu about it. Joshu told them, "Wait a bit and I will go see through the old woman for you." The next day Joshu went to see the old woman and asked her the same question the monks had. The old woman responded the same way to Joshu as she had to the monks. When Joshu got back to the monastery he told the monks, "I have seen through the old woman of Taizan for you."

What did Joshu see when he saw the old woman through and through? He saw her essential nature. He saw the whole universe in the twinkling of her eyes. He saw his own essential nature. In her eyes he saw himself. Each of the monks could have experienced his essential nature right there with the old woman, drinking tea and eating cakes, if his eyes were open.

Though in Joshu's day women were not recognized as Zen teachers, this old woman was wise. The title of this koan could be "An Old Woman Sees Through an Old Man." After all, Joshu began teaching when he was eighty years old so he must have been quite old at the time of this story. When Joshu visited the old woman, she could hold her own with him. Joshu saw her sparkle. He saw her just as she was. This ordinary old woman was extraordinary. There was a lot of life left in her and Joshu and the monks saw her flash it.

Today in our society women are recognized as Zen teachers and their lives sparkle. One day my husband Charles was exhausted from all our Zen travels up and down Route 81. When we arrived at Roshi Richardson's apartment in Baltimore, he flopped down on her sofa and said, "I'm getting too old for all this." Roshi Richardson, in her seventies, flashed him a look he's never forgotten. In that moment Charles saw this wonderful, strong woman through and through.

When I was growing up, there was a famine in Biafra, and my mother's friend went there as a missionary and teacher to help out. At Christmas time my mother sewed dresses and dolls for her friend in Biafra to give to all the little girls in her class. Each dress had a pocket and in the pocket was a little doll that had on a dress just like the little girl's dress. Each dress and matching doll had lace and trim on it exactly alike. As my mother was sitting at her sewing machine working on this project, a neighbor came in and asked her why she was spending so much time on all the trim and detail. After all, the children were so poor they would be happy to have any dress at all and wouldn't know the difference. Mother looked up from her sewing machine and said, "A little girl anywhere in the world can see the difference between a plain dress and a special fancy dress." And at that moment, I saw my mother through and through.

One patient told me, as she was recovering from surgery, that despite the physical discomfort, she felt better than she had in years. The tumor in her abdomen had been removed and she found out that it was not cancerous. She said the experience changed her whole outlook on life. Before her surgery she was worried and depressed about turning forty and dreaded each birthday. Now she sees things differently. She sees each birthday is a precious gift and takes the time to celebrate each one in a special way.

Sitting together silently in meditation helps us see both our sameness and our differences. At the same time we really see and appreciate the uniqueness of each person or thing, we also see the essential nature of each person or thing that is the unity that pervades the universe. We see and appreciate the formless universal in the form of each particular thing.

Seeing does not stop with this insight. Insight motivates you to respond with compassionate action when you see it is needed. Seeing and responding go hand in hand. You need to take time to meditate to clarify and expand your vision, but it doesn't end with sitting and seeing. Zen insight leads you back into the world where you continue to ask, "What do I see?" and "How do I respond?"

# HEARING:

*Responding to What You Hear*

Really listening is an active process. It requires that you pay attention and not be preoccupied with your thoughts and daydreams. In order to listen, you must drop your mental commentary and be fully present. This kind of listening is work. It is the work of a therapist, nurse, social worker, pastor, priest, or rabbi. It is the gift of a true friend. To feel really heard is healing. You no longer feel isolated and alone. Being heard connects you with another human being.

My work as a nurse involves listening to sounds such as breath sounds, heart sounds, and bowel sounds. These are the subtle sounds of life. Their presence, absence, and characteristics speak of the health of organs that cannot be directly seen. And then there are the not-so-subtle sounds of the noisy hospital environment, the paging system, the elevator going up and down, monitors beeping, people talking, and the portable X-ray machine going up and down the hall. Amid all this clatter, you do your best to allow some silence in which to rest and heal.

Lately I've been corresponding with my niece Susan by e-mail. She is the mother of three young children and we enjoy discussing their activities and development. Susan is deaf and I get the feeling that she really enjoys conversing by e-mail because she doesn't have to guess and fill in the gaps. Usually she listens with her eyes through lip-reading and has to guess at many of the letters and words. With e-mail she can hear every word. She is an artist and makes beautiful drawings of infants and children. She also gets great pleasure from photography. Listening transcends hearing. You can listen with all your senses.

Zen is hearing not just with your ears, but with your whole body. Walking past the hedgerow during walking meditation on a hot summer evening, I notice it is alive with insect sounds. I feel the complex rhythm and vibration of hums, buzzes, and chirps.

You can move beyond words and concepts in your hearing. What is the sound of wind if you don't name it? At the shore the wind mixes with the ocean waves. It crashes, swirls, and shakes the house. Here in Radford often when we do walking meditation outside, we hear the sound of cattle mooing as they graze in nearby pastures. What do we hear if we don't dismiss the sound with a word? What is moo?

Zen practice involves profound and subtle listening and hearing. There is a koan that asks, "Who can hear the nonsentient preach the Dharma?" Nonsentient refers to what could be called inanimate objects. One monk worked on this question for a long time and when he finally got it he exclaimed in verse:

> *Wonderful! Wonderful!*
> *The preaching of the Dharma by the nonsentient*
> *is inconceivable.*

*If you try to hear it with your ears, it is hard*
*to understand;*
*When you listen with your mind's eye, then*
*you know it.*

This koan is telling us that even inanimate objects are not lifeless objects. They have a voice and have something to tell us if we know how to listen. The rocks, earth, water, sun, and moon have a message to share. During these times when the ecology of the planet is gravely threatened, it is a message we need to hear. It is a message that reconnects us with the earth and is healing not only for us, but for other creatures and the whole planet as well.

At Christmastime a favorite carol is "Joy to the World." In this song "heaven and nature sing." In one verse, "Fields and floods, rocks, hills and plains repeat the sounding joy." One Christmas, my husband Charles asked our Zen group, "How do the rocks, hills, and plains repeat the sounding joy?" As we sat in the silence of meditation, each of us listened with the mind's eye and the whole body to hear the answer.

One time a monk named Gayasata heard the wind blowing the temple bells and his teacher Sanghanandi asked him, "Are the bells ringing or is the wind ringing?" Gayasata answered, "It is neither the bells nor the wind; it is my Mind that is ringing." Then Sanghanandi asked, "And who is the Mind?" Gayasata replied, "Because both are silent."

Gayasata realized that the silence is the sound. He had

the direct experience that everything is the ringing of Mind. There is no silence apart from the sound. Listening with the mind's eye they are heard simultaneously in each person and thing you encounter.

Kannon is the bodhisattva of compassion. Her name means the one who hears the cries of the world. We need to hear the cries of the world. If we take time to listen, we will hear, and if we truly hear, we will respond compassionately. Zen realization is hearing that heals you and this is actualized in compassionate action that heals others.

Once Zen Master Kyozan was due to give a sermon. He stood up, struck the stand with a gavel, and said, "The Dharma of the Mahayana is beyond the four propositions and transcends the hundred negations. Listen! Listen!" Then he sat down. The monks wondered if he had given a sermon or not.

His words meant that the teaching of Buddha is beyond thoughts, words, and concepts. It cannot be expressed in words or explained intellectually. Therefore he didn't proceed with a lengthy speech.

Kyozan's sermon was the *whack* of the gavel. The direct hearing of *whack* in the present instant was the dharma or reality of the moment. Kyozan urged the monks to listen without the slightest separation from the experience of the sound. Listen to the fact, just this sound, *whack*.

A number of years ago when I traveled from my rural home in Virginia to attend a retreat at an inner-city Zen center, I was amazed to sit in the Zen hall and hear firsthand the sounds of the inner city: sirens, people shouting, and helicopters patrolling overhead. Between sittings we did walking meditation outside among the gardenias and magnolias blooming in the sun-filled gardens around the center grounds. At one point the leader led the line down the walkway between two buildings to do walking meditation in the front yard under the tall palms. Just as we were about to step out from between the two buildings into the front yard, four rapid-fire gunshots rang out at close range. In a split second, at one with the sound, without a thought, the line did an about-face, turning like one body and moved quickly back into the shelter between the two buildings. We were not separate from the sound or from each other. We heard and responded.

One day in another inner city, I made a public health visit to an old woman who had diabetes and needed help caring for an open wound. During the day she baby-sat her little granddaughter Lucille who was a cheerful, talkative four-year-old. While I was talking with the grandmother and dressing the ulcer on her leg, from time to time the silence in the other room was broken with a *whack*. After several *whacks*, the grandmother called out, "Lucille, what are you doing in there?" The little girl called back, "Killin' roaches."

Lucille had one of those little wooden mallets that children use to pound pegs through holes in a board. The board is then turned over and the pegs pounded through in the other direction. It certainly took more concentration and coordination to kill roaches than it did to pound pegs through a board. With each *whack* this little girl demonstrated her resilience, resourcefulness, and confidence as she lived in the reality of her inner-city circumstances. With each *whack* Lucille preached the dharma as profoundly as any Zen master. In each *whack* I heard how a person can be beaten down by life in the inner city. I also heard the call to continue my healing efforts making home visits in her neighborhood.

# EATING:

## Nourishing Yourself and Others

Wholeness is experienced in the everyday acts of your life like eating. When you eat the body is nourished and you are united with the food you eat, the earth where the food was grown, the people who prepared the food, and the people with whom you share the meal. There is a special connection that is experienced around the kitchen table. Often this is the favorite and most used space in the house. This is the place where you eat. It is a sacred place.

When I was in the hospital after surgery I developed a complication called paralytic ileus and couldn't eat for a week. When I got home, I was very weak and could still only eat a clear liquid diet. The day after I got home, my friends Jim and Carol came over and brought me homemade chicken soup and peach Jell-O. The chicken soup tasted so warm and nourishing, and the peach Jell-O cool and refreshing. Sitting at the kitchen table eating chicken soup and Jell-O, I felt life and energy begin to return to my body.

Several years ago, I went to visit a friend who was in the state psychiatric hospital with schizophrenia. Before I went to visit, I called her and asked if there was anything she wanted me to bring to her. She said she was really craving fresh fruit. The hospital food was starting to get to her. She needed something fresh. I went to the grocery store and bought some fresh cantaloupe, honeydew, pineapple, strawberries, and watermelon. I cut up the cantaloupe, honeydew, pineapple, and strawberries and made a bowl of fresh fruit salad. When I got to the hospital, we sat in the sun out in the courtyard and talked while we ate fresh fruit together. We ate large slices of watermelon right down to the rind, spitting the pits onto the grass. It was a moment of freshness, warmth, and human-to-human sharing for me and for my friend.

Sitting with attention morning and evening, in the silence of Zen meditation, increases your awareness of the everyday acts of your life. Zen practice helps you slow down and create the time and space to chew, to taste, and to appreciate the food you eat. When you eat you are present and do not rush through the meal preoccupied with something else. During a Zen retreat, meals are eaten in silence. This helps cultivate an increased awareness of eating. After a retreat, this awareness carries over, influencing the way you experience eating even in the midst of your usual talking and chatter. If you miss the opportunity to experience and enjoy everyday acts like eating, you miss too much of your life.

At one of the first Zen retreats I ever attended, I remember sitting down at the table for breakfast after the early morning meditation period on a cold day in January. As I sat in silence waiting for everyone to get their food, the steam rose from my bowl of oatmeal and I watched the brown sugar melt into a little pool of syrup. When I took the first bite I almost said "mmm" right out loud. Warm oatmeal never tasted so warm and nourishing. Next I peeled and ate an orange and it filled the room with its fresh fragrance. This simple meal was so satisfying and I felt so grateful for it. Eating in silence was a new experience for me that increased my awareness and appreciation for each meal I eat.

Sometimes as a result of health problems, your diet may need to be restricted in some way. This can be very difficult and frustrating, but rather than focusing on foods that are off limits, it may be helpful to pay more attention to foods you can eat. Slow down and really be aware of each bite of your food—its texture, consistency, and flavor. With increased awareness even plain water can be refreshing, satisfying, and flavorful.

One day a monk named Seizei approached Zen Master Sozan and said, "I am solitary and destitute. I beg you, Master, please help me to become prosperous." Zen Master Sozan called out to him, "Venerable Seizei!" and Seizei replied, "Yes, Master." Zen Master Sozan then said, "You have already drunk three cups of the finest Hakka wine and still you say that you have not yet moistened your lips."

Seizei was an advanced monk and had already gained insight through years of Zen practice. In this exchange he was probing Zen Master Sozan for further insight. When Zen Master Sozan calls out to Seizei the presence of Seizei's "yes" shows him that Seizei has already directly experienced the abundance of his essential nature. Zen Master Sozan encourages Seizei to live out the insight in his everyday life because insight alone is not enough; it has to be actualized in daily life.

Zen Master Sozan uses three cups of the finest wine as

an example of savoring and being fully present to life itself. Three cups of the finest wine can also be interpreted
as breakfast, lunch, and dinner. Are you present during
breakfast, lunch, and dinner and do you appreciate the
food you are eating? Or are you solitary and destitute?
Are you preoccupied and separate from the meal and un-
aware of the abundance you have before you?

One common symptom of many different illnesses is
nausea and not being able to eat. You know you are healing
when you are able to eat again. When my nephew Christo-
pher was ten years old, he was hit by a car while he was
riding his bicycle. He was rushed to the hospital by ambulance where he underwent three hours of neurosurgery
to remove bone fragments from his brain. For the next
several days he was on a respirator in the pediatric intensive care unit. He looked like a young alien life form with
his eyes swollen shut, his head wrapped in bandages, and
tubes and wires coming from his mouth, chest, and arms.

One of the first things he said when he regained consciousness was that he wanted some chocolate milk and
Twinkies. Within a few days he was sitting up in bed with
a big smile on his face, a little carton of chocolate milk in
one hand and a Twinkie in the other. He was so happy to
finally be able to eat again. His parents were overjoyed
that he was alive and sitting up in bed eating.

There is so much we take for granted—the ability to
walk, to see, and to hear. Walking, seeing, and hearing
are also three cups of the finest wine that most of us taste
every day. Zen practice cultivates an appreciation for

these everyday miracles in our lives so we can experience
how rich we really are. We do not have to feel alone and
destitute like poor Seizei. We can eat from the abundance
that surrounds us and reach out to share our riches with
those who are in need.

There is a koan that asks, "How do you swallow the
whole Yellow River in one gulp?" With the direct realization of nonseparation and of the unity of life, you see
that each morsel that you eat contains the whole universe.
Each part is one with the whole. Sitting at the kitchen
table, you swallow the whole Yellow River with each
spoonful of food that you eat. You are nourished and
healed as you swallow and realize you are one with all
people, animals, plants, and the whole universe.

The following Zen verse has always been particularly
meaningful to me:

> *Because it is so very clear*
> *It takes long to come to realization*
> *If you know at once that candlelight is fire,*
> *The meal has long been cooked.*

"The meal has long been cooked" means that we are all
already whole. The ordinary acts of your everyday life
are the functioning of wholeness. However, even though
you are already whole, it takes a lot of work to become
aware of your wholeness. You need to wake up and see
that light is light, eating is eating, walking is walking, and
breathing is breathing. When you see this clearly, ordinary life is rich and abundant, and every meal is a feast.

# LAUGHING:

## Sharing Laughter

Laughter eases tension, lifts the spirit, unites those who laugh together, and brightens your outlook on life. Humor has a healing effect on body, mind, and spirit. These days some hospitals offer humor programs for patients who are having chemotherapy or coping with the stress of serious illness. On many pediatric units there is a play therapist who provides play activities and materials appropriate for the children's ages and abilities. At the hospital I see young children riding around and around in the corridor on tricycles with IV poles attached to them. As they ride by, without a pause, they look up at me and we smile and laugh together.

Play and laughter are human needs throughout the life span. Without playfulness and humor, life becomes dry, tedious, and depressing. Play and laughter are spontaneous and involve free movement. When you laugh you shake, throw up your arms, hold your belly, and sometimes you laugh so hard tears roll down your cheeks. When you laugh you are fully present and enjoying the moment.

To be whole you must be willing to embrace the good and the bad, the pleasant and the unpleasant, the funny and the sad. You cannot be attached to a concept or ideal of perfection. You must be willing to take life as it comes and to accept yourself as you are. Humor is healing in that it allows you to laugh at your mistakes and not take yourself too seriously. When you laugh at yourself you acknowledge and embrace your imperfection. This releases you from the great pressure that you place on yourself when you think you must be perfect and never make mistakes.

At a recent Zen retreat a friend, Joseph, served as head monk for the first time. This position involves a lot of work and responsibility. The head monk ensures that the retreat schedule and Zen hall run smoothly so the participants are not distracted and they have an opportunity for deep silence and intense practice. As he was making some heartfelt concluding comments at the end of the retreat, Joseph said, "There are some things I wish I'd have done better and there are some things I wish I hadn't done at all." Joseph and the group had a good laugh at this comment. I think we could all say this about life in general, and realizing this, we can learn, laugh, and move on.

Although Zen looks like serious business with everyone lined up in straight, silent rows in the Zen hall, there is also a long tradition of humor. In one koan two groups of monks were fighting over a cat. Zen Master Nansen came along and saw them arguing and picked up the cat and said, "If one of you can say a word, I will spare the cat. If you can't say anything, I will put it to the sword." None of the monks could come up with an answer so Nansen killed the cat. Later that evening Zen Master Joshu returned to the monastery and Nansen told him about the incident. Joshu took his sandals off his feet, placed them on his head, and walked off. When Joshu did this, Nansen said, "If you had been there, I could have spared the cat."

Of course, the first part of this story is not funny and some have debated whether Nansen really killed the cat or if he just gestured as if to kill the cat. But the point is that the monks were lost in their heads, their thoughts, and their debates and were not able to see and appreciate the cat just as it was. In this sense, they had already killed the cat. Nansen came along and tried to cut off the thoughts, concepts, and opinions that separated them from experiencing life in its fullness. He tried to shake them and wake them up.

The humor comes when Joshu hears about the whole scene and with his action says, "Nonsense. Lighten up boys." The incongruity of placing his sandals on his head is funny and if we had been there we probably would have laughed. Joshu's humor is spontaneous and life giving. The humor, spontaneity, and liveliness of Joshu's response were what they needed to save the cat. Humor, spontaneity, and liveliness not only preserve the life of the cat, but they also breathe life back into all of us.

In the Zen tradition, there is a certain sort of irreverence that is humorous. For example, there is a koan in which a monk comes to Zen Master Unmon and asks him, "What is Buddha?" Unmon responds, "A dried up shit-stick!" You can imagine most sixth grade boys laughing hilariously at this response. This koan is aimed at cutting through dualistic thought like holy and dirty, good and bad, reverent and irreverent. When we see this koan clearly we see that everything is Buddha. Everything is holy and the whole includes the clean and the dirty, the good and the bad.

Practicing Zen does not just mean seeking spiritual development; you must also be willing to be a fool. When working on koans, you go in to see the teacher to present your understanding of the koan. Sometimes you do not see the koan clearly and the teacher sends you off to search more deeply. If you don't maintain a healthy sense of humor, this can be frustrating. Roshi Kennedy once said, "You can't practice Zen if your feelings are easily hurt." Having a good sense of humor and being willing to be the fool or the clown are helpful attitudes to sustain you in Zen practice and in life.

Sometimes our laughter is from sheer joy. It is a Navajo tradition to celebrate the first time a new baby laughs. Likewise, a person's first glimpse of essential nature or wholeness is a joyous occasion and sometimes it is accompanied by a great burst of laughter. One monk was working on the koan, "How is my hand like the Buddha's hand?" When he saw the point of the koan he exclaimed in verse:

> *Groping for the pillow at my back, I could feel it.*
> *In spite of myself, I burst out laughing.*
> *From the first, the whole body is the hand.*

The monk laughed in celebration of oneness.

Laughter unites people who laugh together. One morning I was helping the student nurses get their patients up and bathed and dressed. Then we went to the nurses' station to get the morning medications ready. When we got to the medication room, I noticed that I didn't have my glasses on because I couldn't read the small print on the medication labels. I searched high and low around the nurses' station, but couldn't find my glasses. So I went out onto the unit from room to room retracing my steps. As I made my way down the hallway, I suddenly noticed one of the patients I had helped bathe and dress sitting in his wheelchair outside his door. He was a large rugged man in his seventies who had Alzheimer's disease. There he sat with my little pink glasses on. In surprise I said, "You have my glasses on!" He said, "I do? How did they get there?" We both started laughing and had a really good laugh together as we went to find his glasses and I took my glasses back. Neither of us could remember how the switch took place.

Even in the midst of hard times, laughter can lighten your load. Sharing a good joke with others is humanizing and it unites those who laugh together. Laughter is healing because it relaxes your body, eases your mind, and frees your spirit. When you laugh you let go of your inhibitions and open to the delight of being alive.

# CRYING:

*Sharing Tears*

Sometimes you cry tears of pain, grief, or anguish. Sometimes you cry because you are deeply moved by something very meaningful or beautiful. Sometimes you laugh so hard you cry. When you allow your tears to flow you are free to feel your emotions and to be opened by them.

Sometimes tears are necessary for healing to take place. One day as I was taking care of an elderly woman in the hospital she started to cry and tell me about her husband who had died two years before. She told me how he always sat at the kitchen table in the morning and ate two scrambled eggs, two pieces of toast, and two cups of coffee. Then she cried and said she missed having him at the table with her during breakfast. She told me how he mowed the lawn each week and then came in for a cold drink. Then she cried and said she even missed the grass he tracked into the house on his clothes and shoes. After a while she stopped crying and thanked me for listening to her and for letting her cry. She said that every time she talked about her husband and started to cry, her children would tell her not to cry and would try to cheer her up. She said she needed time to remember and to cry. She said that crying for a while made her feel better, but it made her children too uncomfortable to see her cry.

Each semester I tell my nursing students that one of

the things I want them to learn during their clinical experience is to become comfortable being with a person who is crying. Often new students think they have said something wrong if patients begin to cry and they quickly change the subject and try to cheer them up. Most patients are in the hospital because something sad or difficult is happening in their life and many of them need the opportunity to express their feelings and to cry. Listening to them and being with them while they cry are some of the most caring and healing things you can do. Sometimes you cry with the patient and that can be healing too.

Rachel was a young mother with two little girls, seven and nine years old. She was in the hospital dying of colon cancer. She had tried every treatment her doctors recommended, but her cancer advanced. Each day I helped her put on a clean nightie and fix her hair and make-up just before her husband and children came to see her. She conserved what little energy she had for her family's visit each afternoon. Her husband adored Rachel and the little girls and was completely devastated by her illness. After they went home each day, Rachel cried because she wouldn't be there to help her husband raise the girls. When Rachel died, her husband and parents were there at her bedside crying. Tears flowed from the eyes of her oncologist and nurses too. They had all done everything they could and still Rachel died. Through our tears we acknowledged the tremendous loss that Rachel's death was and for each of us tears were the beginning of the process of healing from this loss.

When we practice Zen, we become more sensitive and aware of both the pain and the exquisite beauty in the world. Rather than trying to embrace the beauty and exclude or push away what is painful, we come face to face with both; as a result we come face to face with the whole just as it is. We feel both the pain and the joy of life and we are free to respond with all of our humanity.

Hsueh-tou studied with Zen Master Tsung-chueh. One day Tsung-chueh was giving a talk about the life of the Buddha's successor Kasyapa and he said, "Buddha spoke with a hidden meaning, but it was not concealed to Kasyapa." When Hsueh-tou heard these words, he was greatly awakened. He stood there in the crowd with tears running down his face and said, "Why haven't I heard this before?"

For the first time Hsueh-tou experienced the meaning of the words that he had heard so many times before. He directly experienced his essential nature, unity, nonseparation. Seeing clearly that which had previously been hidden from his view, was so moving that he stood there in the crowd with tears of emotion flowing from his eyes.

Often there is a great emotional release of tears or laughter to see for the first time what was right there all the time. There can be a feeling of sadness that one searched so hard for years and years to finally see what was right here all along. One wonders, "Why wasn't I aware of this all along? Why did I have to wait so long to be able to see this?" For some people there is the urge to laugh as if a great joke had been played on them. Tears of laughter run from their eyes as they finally get the punch line. Some people alternately laugh and cry at the sheer joy, freedom, and beauty of the experience. Some cry tears of gratitude for the experience and for the teachers who encouraged them along the way.

I was fortunate to study with Roshi Kennedy who often can be seen crying while listening to a moving Zen talk. In many ways he's a very macho man partly as a result of many years of disciplined Jesuit training. But he is also a very caring and sensitive man who is not afraid to let his feelings show. For me his tears are healing because they show me that he is a whole person with the full range of human emotion.

Several years ago one of our nursing students died in a tragic accident. Many of the nursing students and several faculty members drove several hours out into the mountains to the small town where the funeral and burial took place. During the service the pastor said, "What do we do when a tragedy like this happens? We do what Jesus did when his friend Lazarus died. Jesus wept." Through my tears I saw three rows of young women sitting in front of me crying their eyes out because their friend was dead. After the funeral service, we gathered for the burial in a little cemetery on a hilltop overlooking ridge after ridge of rolling hills. The tears of the family and friends were one with the green grasses, the dogwoods, and the redbuds of that late April afternoon in the mountains of West Virginia. In our shared expression of sorrow, we were united and comforted by each other and by the beauty of nature all around us.

Often during a Zen retreat, when we sit for many periods of meditation, people get in touch with their pain and separation. When people come to see me in individual meetings, often they bring me their pain. One person's father just died. One person is going through a difficult divorce. One person's child is in trouble. One person has a life-threatening illness. Many people cry and sometimes I cry with them. Sometimes that's all there is, just tears.

# INTIMACY:
## Sharing Your Whole Self

Taped to my refrigerator is a quote by Maezumi Roshi that I cut out of a Zen Center of Los Angeles newsletter years ago. It means as much to me today as it did when I first read it. It says, "In your daily life, please accept yourself as you are and your life as it is. Be intimate with yourself . . . I want you to take good advantage of every chance you have to become a really intimate being."

When you are intimate with yourself you accept and get to know who you really are deep down. When you are intimate with others you feel free to share who you really are and to say what you think. You feel free to let down your guard. Roshi Kennedy speaks of the beautiful undefended self. With intimate friends you are free to be your beautiful undefended self. Your intimate friends know and accept you just as you are. Intimacy helps you to be the whole human being that you already are. Intimacy allows the other person to be whole also. Intimacy unites and heals both self and others.

Everyday life is full of opportunities to be an intimate human being each moment. Some experiences in life are especially powerful in teaching us to be intimate, like birth, falling in love, and death. Many women describe giving birth to their children as the most mystical, spiritual, intimate experience of their lives. Birth is a very intimate experience for many men as well. In describing his experience in the delivery room when our daughter was born, my husband Charles said, "She was closer to me than I was to myself."

When most people think of the word intimacy they think of falling in love and being sexually intimate. Falling in love and making love carry you beyond your usual boundaries and way of experiencing life. The senses are more vivid and alive and you are filled with a wonderful joy and energy. You experience yourself, your lover, and your life more intimately.

Death also teaches you intimacy. As a nurse, bathing, feeding, and helping a dying person breathe, move, and sleep comfortably is very intimate. I experience that this is another human being just like me. We all need to breathe, eat, drink, move, and go to the bathroom. We all feel pain and we all die. It is also an intimate experience because of the palpable feeling in the room when someone is dying or has just died.

Zen practice helps you be intimate with yourself, to know who you are, and to know the ground you stand on. At the same time you don't know who you are. There is always something new to find out. So you make friends with the wonder and the mystery that you are.

During Zen meditation you get to know your body intimately. After a long day of sitting in meditation at a Zen retreat, you know every muscle, ache, or pain in your body. You watch as sensations arise, build to great intensity, and then dissipate. You feel your breath deep in your belly. You become intimate with your heart, guts, hands, knees, and feet, instead of residing only in your head. You accept and make friends with your body just as it is moment to moment.

During Zen meditation you get to know your mind intimately. Sitting in meditation hour after hour you see how your mind works. You see the same stories, thoughts, concerns, worries, and plans pass through your mind over and over again until you are sick of them. With awareness and not clinging to them or adding to them, you see some of them lose their grip and dissolve. You see how your mind works. You see through to the nature of mind, to Big Mind.

Many times I've noticed that I have become absorbed in a conflict at work or a family crisis that arises and my mind races thinking about who said what or planning what I should do next. Sitting down to meditate and letting go of worrying and planning for twenty-five minutes, broadens my perspective and gets me in touch with Big Mind. It is like listening to the music of a great composer. The composer must have opened to Big Mind to be able to write the piece. Hearing it opens the listener to something larger. It moves you deeply and calls you to be the best human being you can be. You become intimate with the essence of who you are and the essence of all creation.

There is a koan about intimacy. Once a monk named Buddhamitra asked his teacher Buddhanandhi the following question in verse:

*Father and mother are not close to me;*
*With whom am I most intimate?*
*The Buddhas are not my Way;*
*With what Way am I most intimate?*

Buddhanandhi responded:

*Your speech is one with your [intrinsic] Mind,*
*And not even your mother and father can compare*
*[in closeness].*
*Your actions are one with the Way,*
*And this is what the Mind of Buddhas is.*

Your own mind is Big Mind and is most intimate. There is no need to search elsewhere. Your own way is the Way. Your own life, just as it is, is the life to live out fully. It is your own beautiful, intimate life.

Once when Charles and I were attending a conference in Switzerland with Roshi Kennedy, a young man from Japan who was the attendant of a Japanese Zen master, sat across the table from us at dinner. He watched with great interest as Charles, Roshi Kennedy, and I joked, teased, and conversed during the meal. Toward the end of the meal, he asked Charles and me, "Are you Roshi Kennedy's students or his friends?" We answered that we were both. He said, "But that is not possible!" and continued to watch the intimate interaction taking place before his eyes. When I became a Zen teacher, Roshi Kennedy said to me, "Now you are no longer my student. You are my friend." We are surely friends, but also I will always be his student.

My best friend growing up was Karen who lived across the street. Karen used to get so excited by the beauty and life force of a tree that she would run up, put her arms around it, and give the tree a big hug. Karen and I are still close friends. This past summer we shared an intimate moment. We stood out at the edge of a field together in the bright sunshine of an early August morning picking blackberries and eating them straight from the branch. The evening before we had talked for hours catching up on the past year's events. Now we were silent—united with each other and one with the earth. The moment was complete and vibrant and there was no need for words.

At one time I helped lead a support group for hospitalized teenagers. One day as I arrived on the unit to round up the teens and get the group underway, the first person I saw was a young teenage boy standing by the elevator. He was crying, holding his father's arm, and begging him not to go. His father's eyes filled with tears as he explained that he had to leave now in order to get to work on time. I invited the boy to come with me to get the other teens together for group and he did.

During the group, he explained that he had cancer and that it had spread. He said the group reminded him of the camp he had attended the previous summer for kids with cancer. He had some really fun times at camp, made close friends, and missed the closeness and special feeling of being there. Hearing this, an older boy in the group invited him to come to his room to visit anytime. The two boys became close friends during their hospital stay, openly sharing their hopes, dreams, fears, pain, jokes, and youth. Intimacy is the freedom to be and to share your whole self with others and freeing others to do the same.

# FREEDOM:

## Liberating Yourself and Others

Each of us needs the freedom to be healed in our own way. Too much unsolicited advice is a hindrance rather than help. As a caregiver, you can listen, empathize, provide information, and provide resources, but you cannot make another feel whole. They are free to take that step or leap in their own good time. When you let go of the urge to control others, even for their own good, you free yourself and at the same time you free others too.

I remember going to a retreat once, and at the end of the retreat a man said that during the retreat he had set down some heavy baggage that he had been carrying around for a long, long time. He couldn't believe how much better he felt. He said he was traveling a lot lighter now and felt freer and more energetic.

Sometimes you actually get a sore neck, shoulders, and back because you are carrying the weight of the world on your shoulders. You can learn from the younger generation and ask yourself, "Who died and left you in charge?" Can you let it go? Take a deep breath and let it go. With each exhalation release the tension in your neck, back, and shoulders. With each breath, become lighter and freer. In all of this I think you can see that it is your clinging and trying to control that binds you. Loosen your grip. Breathe freely.

Once a monk named Ta-i, bowed to Zen Master Chien-chih, and said, "I beg you in your great compassion to give me the teaching of liberation." Chien-chih replied, "Who is binding you?" The monk said, "No one is binding me." Chien-chih asked, "Then why are you seeking liberation?" With these words the monk was greatly awakened. The teacher's asking "Who is binding you?" led the student to realize that no one was binding him. Therefore, if he was feeling bound it was because he was binding himself. How do you bind yourself?

Often you have many expectations of yourself. You don't accept yourself just as you are. You have many expectations for your life. Often you don't accept your life just as it is. During Zen meditation you lay down the weight of your expectations and accept each moment just as it is. To let go and lay down the burden of your expectations is healing.

Many people on a spiritual path have the expectation that they will not get anxious or angry and that life will always be pleasant and peaceful. But anxiety, anger, and conflict are a part of life. Getting upset that you are anxious or angry or that conflict has arisen only adds fuel to the fire. Seeing these emotions and situations as a part of life and being aware of them in the present moment, rather than denying them or feeling guilty about them, frees you to face and respond to your circumstances with all your energy and resources. Awareness helps you see and choose the best course of action.

Being whole includes all of your emotions and all of

life's circumstances. Your energy is not consumed by blocking off aspects of your self and of life. You are free to embrace the whole.

The most well-known collection of koans is the *Mumonkan*. *Mumonkan* is often translated into English as *Gateless Gate*. This name implies that there is no barrier, nothing blocking us. We are free right here and now. We don't have freedom. We are freedom. There is a beautiful verse in Zen Master Mumon's Preface to the *Mumonkan:*

> *Gateless is the Great Tao,*
> *There are thousands of ways to it.*
> *If you pass through this barrier,*
> *You may walk freely in the universe.*

If there is no gate or barrier, what does Zen free you from? Zen frees you from your head. It frees you from your constant thinking, figuring, worrying, planning, and controlling. It frees you from the constraints of linear logic. There is a Zen saying, "When a carp in the eastern sea is struck with a stick, it rains torrents as though a tray of water is overturned." You are free to make great leaps of logic and open to your intuitive faculties.

Roshi Kennedy once said, almost as a warning, "When Zen frees you, you are free indeed." Zen frees you from the walls you have built around yourself. You build walls to defend yourself and for protection, but they wall you off from others and the world. You feel separate and lonely. With regular Zen practice, one day the walls come down. They crumble and utterly collapse. You realize that you are incredibly free.

While working as a nurse on a general psychiatry unit, many days most of my patients were depressed and suicidal. The most effective treatment currently available for these patients is a combination of antidepressant medication and cognitive therapy. Cognitive therapy is based on the principle that how we feel and behave is affected by the thoughts we think. Distorted or irrational thoughts lead to difficult feelings and problematic behaviors.

Marsha Linehan has combined cognitive-behavioral therapy with insights she gained from her study and practice of Zen to develop dialectical behavior therapy. She developed this approach from extensive work with people who are suicidal and people with borderline personality disorder. Many therapists find these people too frustrating to work with, but Linehan maintains a hopeful stance, grounded in the total acceptance of the person and their responses, at the same time amplifying their strengths and capabilities. In an atmosphere of total acceptance and validation, they feel the challenge and freedom to change.

You need to see what is binding you, experience that you are already free, and learn how to live free. Think of an animal, a lion or a bear, that was raised in captivity. When it comes time for its release back into the wilderness, it has to learn how to live free. It needs practice and training. For human beings Zen meditation is practice for living free. You sit in silence and drop your habitual ways of thinking, your preconceived ideas, and your preoccupations. This frees the mind.

One time I was getting more and more aggravated with a student nurse who came late to the hospital three times in a row even though I had reminded her of the importance of being on time. When she arrived late for the fourth time, I read her the riot act. At this time she shared with me that her brother was terminally ill and she was the only person he had to help him. Hearing her story, my perception of this student shifted immediately and I was freed from being angry with her. Instead I felt compassion and we talked about the need to notify others when you need to be late and about resources to help her and her brother. We were both freed and experienced healing in our interaction that morning.

You are free to change your mind. You are free to be who you are and to accept others as they are. You are free to marvel and wonder at the incredible intricacy of each creature, to see the mountains dance, and to explore the universe. You are free to work compassionately for others who need justice, peace, or healing.

# COMMUNITY:

*Supporting One Another*

We are not isolated individuals. We are one with a vast interdependent universe. The word community means "with unity." The direct experience of unity or whole-ness is healing and brings us back into harmony with the community in which we live. When we experience this kind of healing, we perceive and feel at home in the larger global community as well. We feel supported by the community and in turn we support others through compassionate action.

Our culture overemphasizes autonomy and individu-ality. Although these are important aspects of human ex-perience, if not balanced with an understanding of our interdependence with other people, many feel alienated, isolated, and lonely. Without a deep understanding of our dependence on the earth, atmosphere, plants, and animals, we become cut off from our roots, body, breath, and spirit.

Living on the Navajo reservation for several years helped me to see that there are alternative views regard-ing autonomy and individuality. The Navajos experience themselves as inseparable from their clan, tribe, and land. In the classroom, if one of the students answered a ques-tion incorrectly, the other students would not raise their hands to give the correct answer. They would not try to outdo one another in this way. Knowledge and wisdom were sought not for the spiritual development of the individual, but rather to benefit the people. I was fortunate to be invited to attend many Navajo sings which healed individuals by bringing them back into harmony with the community and with nature.

When I first began my career as a nurse, many hospitals were community hospitals. They were nonprofit organizations formed to meet the health care needs of the people in the community. Now more and more of our hospitals are corporations where the bottom line is money. Viewing the hospital as a business is an example of the highly individualistic nature of our society. The business model has not been successful in meeting the health care needs of the people. There is a need to balance financial considerations and individual profit with consideration of the good of the community and the need for humanitarian service. Community is an integral part of health and healing.

Experiencing a connection with other people heals isolation and loneliness. Many people who are seriously ill, very old, or dying, feel isolated, cut off from the mainstream of life. They long to remain fully integrated into the community and to feel a connection with other people. We connect with others not only by giving, but also by being willing to receive and listen to others. We in turn must be willing to express our needs and feelings. Through listening to and sharing with one another, relationships are formed and we feel closeness and connection.

Each semester my nursing students and I participate in a day of adventure-based learning. One of the exercises we do is to have one person at a time lie down on the floor. The rest of the group lifts her up over their heads and she remains reclining in the air above them for a few moments. Then they return her gently to the floor. This experience is interesting both for the lifter and the one being lifted. As the lifter, you learn that with enough help even a large person can be lifted without straining your back. It reinforces the need to call for help when lifting a patient rather than proceeding alone and suffering a back injury. For the person being lifted, it is a direct experience of what it is like to trust others and to be upheld by the group. This is a very moving and healing experience for many individuals.

One facet of community is working as a team. The sophisticated treatments and technology that have been developed require that teams of health care providers work together. Several years ago my brother had open-heart surgery to replace a defective valve in his heart. He was amazed by how smoothly and efficiently the nurses, doctors, and technicians worked as a team to keep him as comfortable as possible before, during, and after the surgery. He said his open-heart surgery was less painful than a dental procedure he had had the year before to repair a tooth.

One colleague tells me that the high point of her career as a nurse is when the doctors and nurses in the emergency room work together like a well-oiled machine. When a person who was in an accident arrives by ambulance at the emergency room, each trauma team member quickly moves into action doing just what he or she is supposed to do. They flow together, working effectively, to save the person's life. There is a sense of unity and of being part of something larger than yourself. Together they accomplish what they could not accomplish alone.

Community is an important aspect of Zen practice. When you attend a Zen retreat this is readily apparent. Everyone follows the same schedule, rising together early in the morning. Everyone sits silently together during round after round of meditation. Between rounds of sitting, the meditators line up close behind one another and do walking meditation. Walking in the meditation line, the group moves like one body, like the body of a centipede with many legs. During work periods everyone works together in silence and three times a day everyone silently eats meals together.

A Zen retreat is not like many retreats where people relax, read, and take walks on their own schedule. A Zen retreat is a group effort. Each person must sit and experience for him or herself, but at the same time each person supports the others in a weekend or week of intensive Zen practice. Everyone is expected to sit each scheduled period of meditation. An individual does not decide to take a nap instead. The community supports one another in being present and awake.

Sometimes without saying a word you feel very close with others. When attending a Zen retreat, as the days go by you feel a special closeness and appreciation for the other people participating in the retreat even though nobody says anything. When a group gets together to practice Zen meditation once a week, closeness is cultivated by the silent sitting as much as by the words shared before or after. In silence, the deep all-pervading unity is perceived.

Through Zen practice you wake up to the direct experience that you are not separate. At the same time you see that you are completely alone, in that there is no other. The dualistic opposition of self and other, autonomy and dependence, aloneness and community are transcended. The individual is not a thing, nor is the community a thing. We are simultaneously not the same and not different. You are an individual living in community.

Our Zen group chose its name, New River Zen Community because we experience a sense of community as we sit and walk together in silence and because we support one another in our commitment to practice Zen. Especially when a person is first learning Zen meditation, it is easier to sit with a group than all by yourself. Although we are a Zen community, we do not seek to establish ourselves as a separate community. We are fully integrated into the many communities in which we live our lives. Whatever we realize through Zen practice is actualized in the way we live our lives in our families, our workplaces, and in local and global communities. Roshi Kennedy often challenges his Zen students by saying, "Who cares about your enlightenment, if it doesn't lead to compassionate action?" Any authentic enlightenment experience leads us back into our communities. It does not isolate us. The energy of our insight is poured back into building up and healing our families, our workplaces, and our local and global communities.

# SERVICE:
## *Doing What Needs to Be Done*


In serving others you yourself are healed. Service is more than doing for another. In being with, doing with, and doing for others, you experience the deep unity that you share with others. The boundaries and barriers between self and others dissolve and you feel connected and whole. From the experience of unity and wholeness springs genuine service. Genuine service helps you continue to grow in your awareness of wholeness.

As a nurse, I entered a profession with a long tradition of providing humanitarian service both in times of war and in times of peace. In both war and peace, the human need for care during disease, old age, and death is ever present. Although today many nurses find themselves working in health care agencies that are organized like businesses aimed at maximizing profit, they continue to try to integrate a humanitarian service perspective aimed at helping people, alleviating suffering, and improving quality of life. Many jobs can be viewed as service to humanity and the earth. Teachers, electricians, engineers, social workers, carpenters, artists, and geologists can all work with a spirit of integrity, generosity, and service. When you use your life energy for service, your work is healing for self and others.

There is a koan that says, "Even Shakyamuni and

Maitreya are servants of that one. Just tell me, who is that one?" Shakyamuni is the historical Buddha and Maitreya is the future Buddha. So this koan is telling us that even Buddha is a servant of something greater than himself. For all times past, present, and future, it is essential to be a servant.

This koan is asking, "Who do you serve?" It is asking, "Who is that one?" A person from a theistic tradition like Christianity, Judaism, or Islam might have a ready answer to this question. But the Zen approach encourages you to look, inquire, and experience rather than formulate a verbal answer. There is a Zen verse that says, "He now is surely me, but I am not Him." "That one" is larger than yourself and at the same time not other than yourself and others.

Yamada Roshi spoke of four types of people: an ordinary person without enlightenment, an ordinary person with enlightenment, a saint without enlightenment, and a saint with enlightenment. Of course, the fourth type is what we would all like to be and what the world needs most. However, what this scheme is pointing out is that personal insight and saintly action in the world do not necessarily go hand in hand. Insight alone is not enough. Insight must be coupled with an ongoing effort to actualize in your actions what you have realized through meditation practice. Insight is actualized through service.

In the Buddhist tradition, a bodhisattva is a person who has realized his or her true nature and rather than entering nirvana or heaven, remains in the world to help others until everybody and everything realizes its true nature. This involves helping everybody and everything to see how beautiful they really are and to live their lives accordingly. One day as I was exercising on an indoor track, I watched a group of young men shooting baskets on the basketball court below. They were in constant motion, running, jumping, and bouncing basketballs across the shiny wooden floor. They were thoroughly enjoying all the action and interaction. They appeared before me as ten big-footed bodhisattvas, dressed in brightly colored tank tops and baggy shorts. They were just being themselves and beckoning to me to enjoy the sheer color and movement of being alive.

There are many types of service. Zen literature contains examples of Zen students who served in the role of attendant to their Zen teacher, such as Ananda serving as Buddha's attendant and Ejo serving as Dogen's attendant. Ananda and Ejo served their teachers so their teachers would be free to teach. In time, Ananda and Ejo became teachers themselves and continued to serve, giving generously of their time and talents to provide others with the opportunity to practice and study Zen. I have often thought that my career in nursing is like being a professional attendant meeting the needs of others so they have time to heal.

Once Zen Master Unmon said to the monks, "The world is vast and wide. Why do you put on your seven-piece robes at the sound of the bell?" Once you have directly experienced your essential nature and the vast unbounded universe opens before you, you are free. Why do you put on your robe and continue to serve? Why do you do anything? Why do you serve? It is when you are free that true service can emerge. True service is offered freely without any expectation of reward or return. There is no attachment to the outcome of the service. The service is offered realizing that sometimes you cannot fix things. You simply see what needs to be done and do it with integrity and generosity. You simply see who needs a companion and you are present person to person.

When my father was a little boy, about eight years old, he got a terrible illness called St. Vitus' dance. It attacked his nervous system and he lost control of all his muscles. He lost the ability to walk, talk, and feed himself. Luckily, he recovered from this illness and went on to become an engineer, to get married, and to raise a family. However, the recovery process was slow and difficult. It took him about two years to learn all over again how to walk, dress himself, and write. During this time, when he went out to play with the other children, he was slow and spastic. The kids teased him and called him Uncle Wiggly. When they ran off to play, he couldn't keep up and was often left behind crying. They all ran off except for one little girl who always waited for him. She tied his shoes for him so he wouldn't trip and walked along slowly with him until he caught up. What did the little girl see that the other children did not? Why did she stay behind to help him? Who did she serve?

When we realize that we are whole and not separate

from others, all of our actions, both large and small, can be viewed as service. Serving as a family caregiver may require small actions done with sensitivity and generosity of spirit like driving someone to a doctor's appointment, cooking a meal, or running an errand. Or caregiving may require courageous acts of assuming the long-term responsibility for providing and coordinating the twenty-four-hour-a-day care of an ill family member. For some people circumstances will allow them to serve people in their community or in another country. However the opportunity for service presents itself in your life, it is a way to embrace and express your wholeness and the oneness of life by doing what needs to be done one moment at a time.

# PEACEMAKING:
## *Let Peace Begin with Me*

When you are feeling whole and healed you are at peace with yourself and with your life just as it is. You are able to face the circumstances of life and you have the energy to do what needs to be done in your own life and to work for justice and peace in the world.

Peacemaking is important in both life and death. Recently, a local businessman died after a long painful illness due to cancer that had metastasized to multiple sites throughout his body. I knew him before he became ill and I remembered him telling me that he had been in Japan on business in the seventies and had gone to the Zen temples in Kamakura while he was there. He said he was so impressed with the wisdom and peace of mind of the Zen masters he met there. One spring when Roshi Kennedy was coming to Virginia to give a Zen retreat, I invited this man to come and join us. He said that it was wonderful that we were having a Zen retreat right here in Radford and that he would really like to come, but that his hearing was very poor these days and he was in too much pain to sit in meditation. Then he said, in a tone of voice that I will never forget, "All this is happening too late for me."

As his illness progressed, hospice nurses came to his home to help manage his pain and to assist his wife and family. He was a deeply spiritual man and approached his death peacefully. As the time of his death drew near, he made the request that the people at his funeral sing the song, "Let there be peace on earth, and let it begin with me." He died peacefully at home surrounded by family and friends.

Once a monk named Eka approached Zen Master Bodhidharma and said, "Your disciple's mind is not at peace. I beg you master, give it rest." Bodhidharma replied, "Bring your mind to me and I will put it to rest." Eka went off and meditated, searching diligently for his mind, and when he returned he said to Bodhidharma, "I have searched for the mind but have never been able to find it." Bodhidharma replied, "I have finished putting it to rest for you."

As a result of Zen practice, what do you find out about the mind itself? You find that the mind itself is empty. It is not a thing. It is not separate from the whole universe. This insight brings great peace. Some people do not reach this experience of great peace because they are afraid or not willing to loosen their grip on their opinions, expectations, and separateness. If you look your fear right in the face and with great determination let go of your habitual ways of thinking, peace will come.

Peace does not deny anger or conflict. Anger and conflict arise in the course of everyday life. Peace has to do with how you respond to anger and conflict. Sitting in meditation morning and evening day after day, you see various emotions such as anger rise and fall. You learn to move with the emotions as if you were surfing on the waves of a great ocean. Through this process of increasing awareness of how the mind and emotions function, you become less reactive to upsetting situations. You have more flexibility and presence of mind to choose how to respond rather than quickly jumping into the fire.

The decreased reactivity and increased calmness and peace gained through meditation can be extended to others around you. When conflict and crisis arise you are better able to remain calm and take time to listen to the other person's perspective before responding. Experiencing nonseparation and the unity of life does not mean sameness. But rather it brings with it an appreciation for the uniqueness of each individual and the tremendous differences among us. Having let go of your attachment to set opinions and expectations you not only tolerate, but actually respect and enjoy, differences. You are better able to agree to disagree and continue to work together for the common good.

Being peaceful does not mean you are passive or bland. There is a sentence describing Zen Master Dogen that says, "Liberated, he is mild and peaceful, and the thunder roars." People who are at peace are not afraid to speak out about how they see things and to act to achieve justice and peace. They are as peaceful as a lamb but can roar like a lion.

Sitting together in silent meditation is one way to work toward justice and peace. Many times I have attended interreligious conferences that brought together people from different countries, cultures, and religions.

Sitting together in silent meditation at the beginning of the day cultivated a deep sense of unity and shared humanity that transcended the presentations and discussions that took place during the remainder of the time. The shared silence of meditation provided a foundation for deeper dialogue among the participants throughout the day. Both the silence and the talking were essential elements that led to joint action to meet the pressing needs for justice and the healing of conflict.

Peacemaking, like healing, is an ongoing process. You are challenged to continuously make peace with yourself while simultaneously extending that peace to the people around you and to the world.

Last year at a Zen Peacemaker Order retreat that I attended, Claude AnShin Thomas, who is a priest and dharma holder in the Zen Peacemaker Order, told about his experience as a soldier in Vietnam. During his service in Vietnam he killed over two hundred people. Later on when he returned to the United States he became depressed and suicidal. Eventually, he returned to Vietnam to walk across the countryside on a peacemaking mission. Next he was planning to walk across the United States on a peacemaking mission and give retreats for veterans and others interested in peacemaking.

Toward the end of the retreat, I was talking with Claude and I told him that each week I go with my nursing students to the local Veterans Hospital and we take care of patients on the acute psychiatry unit. The students learn so much and see for themselves the wounds of war that are still in need of healing. It's hard work, but the students and I have a great experience there because the veterans express so much gratefulness and appreciation for our care and attention. I asked Claude to keep us and the nurses and patients at the Veterans Hospital in his prayers on his upcoming peacemaking walk. He said, "I always do, but now I have a face to go with it." Later on as we were leaving the retreat, Claude waved and called out to me, "Take good care of my boys." I called back, "I will."

# COMPASSION:
## Creating an Ocean of Compassion

Compassion, acceptance, respect, kindness, and love for self are the foundation for compassionate action in the world. When you are awake you realize your wholeness, you hear the cries of the world, and you see that you are free to respond. When you directly experience that we are one body, you are moved to care for self, others, and the great earth.

In some traditions, self-denial has been emphasized, and as a result, it is very difficult for some people to extend compassion, acceptance, respect, kindness, and love to themselves. In this context, Roshi Kennedy once said, "It is easier to free other people, than it is to free yourself." Yet you must respect, love, and care for yourself in order to respect, love, and care for those you are trying to help because there is no separation between self and others.

If you focus only on the needs of others, your attempts at compassionate action can lead to burnout and codependence. In codependence, your life becomes dependent on helping others to the point of neglecting your own needs and development. The others are viewed as being dependent on your help and their autonomy, ability, and responsibility are undermined. This helping is out of balance. It is helping based on separation between self and other. Compassionate action that is balanced springs forth from the ability to love the self that is not separate from others. The same generosity, gentleness, forgiveness, and kindness that are extended to others are also extended to yourself.

Buddha used the analogy of a fine horse that runs at the mere shadow of the whip to describe four types of people. The fine horse is like the first type of person who feels and responds to the death of someone in another village. The second horse won't run until its hair is touched by the whip. This is like people who feel and respond to a death in their own village. The third horse won't run until the whip touches its hide. This is like people who don't respond until the death is in their own family. The fourth horse won't run until the whip touches its bones. This refers to the people who feel and respond only when they themselves are faced with life-threatening illness.

You don't need to wait until you have a life-threatening illness to begin the healing process. Like the fine horse, you can become more aware of your wholeness and become more sensitive to the healing needed in yourself and in the world right now. Daily practice of Zen meditation is one way to open, sensitize, and nurture yourself so you can be a healing presence in the world.

A friend told me that when he first started Zen meditation he couldn't believe how wonderful it felt to take a break from all the demands of his job and family life and enjoy some quiet time sitting in silence. He said his meditation time was a much-needed gift to himself and that it also helped him become more sensitive and aware of the needs of others. He said that one day he was at the mall with his wife and young son. As they passed through a department store, his wife stopped to look through a rack of sweaters that caught her eye. Their little boy started pulling at her pant leg to get her attention. Ordinarily my friend would have rushed his wife along or left by himself saying she could meet him at the bookstore when she was done. But this time he saw his wife's need to have some relaxing time by herself trying on sweaters and browsing for a new outfit so he took his son by the hand and they went off to throw pennies into the fountain while his wife took her time.

Being compassionate to yourself and those closest to you is the foundation for being truly compassionate to others in the world. Compassionate action is the natural response or the fruit of experiencing your true nature. At the root of compassionate action is the deep experience of nonseparation, unity, and oneness of life. Simultaneously you experience that there is no separate self and self is expanded to include everything.

When you perceive that you are not separate from others or from the earth, you want to care for others and for the earth just as you care for your own body. Your body does not end with your skin. It co-extends with the whole universe. The experience of nonseparation or unity is not an abstraction, it is experienced in the particular realities that surround you. The body makes demands. It gets hungry, thirsty, cold, and sometimes sick.

To respond compassionately to the body, you must respond with food, water, clothing, shelter, and health care.

The Corporal Works of Mercy—to feed the hungry, give drink to the thirsty, clothe the naked, visit the imprisoned, shelter the homeless, care for the sick, and bury the dead—are so named because they are carried out by the body, for the body, the one body. You respond in practical ways to the everyday needs of the people and of the earth. This is the fact of compassionate action. This is love in action.

There is a Zen koan about love. One day a monk said to Zen Master Tung-an Tao-pi, "The ancients said, 'What worldly people love, I love not.' I wonder what you love." To this Zen Master Tung-an Tao-pi replied, "I have already been able to be like this."

When the ancient Zen masters said that they did not love what worldly people love they were referring to the love of people and things as separate objects. Most people perceive that there is a separation between the subject and the object, between the lover and what is loved. The master's response indicated a kind of love that saw the oneness of lover and loved. His was a kind of love that did not cling, but rather was free to move with the fluidity of the present moment. In his response he did not use the word love because he did not want us to be one step removed from the actual experience. He did not want us to get stuck in the concept of love or the concept of compassion. He wanted love to heal us and free us to be truly compassionate human beings moment by moment.

During a recent Zen retreat a man in his early thirties named David came for an individual meeting. His question to me was "How do you live with cancer?" His lips quivered and he struggled to hold back tears as he told me about his wife who was being treated for Hodgkin's disease. I told him that you cry and allow the tears to pour out. I said that you "be with" your wife, express your feelings to each other, and face what is happening with all of your resources.

David said he came to see me because of the talk I had given earlier that day. Roshi Kennedy had introduced me and told the retreat participants that when I became a Zen teacher he gave me the name Jikai, which means Ocean of Compassion, because I work as a nurse and often tell stories about nursing in the retreat talks that I give. David asked me to write down the name Jikai on a piece of paper for him because he wanted to go back and see the nurses who worked on the unit where his wife had recently received a bone marrow transplant. He said the nurses knew just what they were doing and treated him and his wife so compassionately that he wanted them to have this name.

Ocean of Compassion is a name that I gladly share with all nurses. It is a name that all human beings can aspire to. It is a name that reminds me each day what is most important to attend to and live out. We are all already oceans of compassion. If you wake up this moment to your wholeness, the abundance you realize will overflow in compassionate action.

# Epilogue:
## Awakening to Healing

Healing begins right where you are right now. The first step, like the last step, is to be compassionate to yourself. As you experience healing, you embody healing and can extend a truly healing hand to others. As you heal, you will find that you become more open to learning from every situation and more accepting of a healing hand from others. The hand that gives and the hand that receives are one hand.

Life is incredibly rich and full if you are open to the whole of life. The whole of life includes illness, loss, pain, anger, fear, and death. When you try to wall yourself off from these aspects of life, you become separate and suffer in isolation. When you let down the walls and embrace all of life, you see that you are larger than you think. This realization is enlivening, healing, and full of possibility. A life of wholeness is not always easy or pleasant, but it is vital, boundless, and compassionate.

Zen is not an attempt to fix or perfect yourself. It is a call to awaken and see your own true nature that is whole and one with everything. Although a book like this can serve as an invitation to wholeness that opens your mind and whets your appetite, reading and thinking about Zen is not enough. Zen, like healing, must be embodied. Sitting in meditation opens you to directly experience wholeness and healing in body, mind, and spirit. You awaken to the realization that body, mind, spirit, and the whole universe are one. Awakening to wholeness, you are freed and energized to step forth in compassionate action. Meditation and compassionate action complement each other and enable you to live a life that simultaneously heals yourself, others, the earth, and all beings— for we are one.

# An Introduction to Zen Practice

You may want to try Zen practice by following the instructions that follow or by attending an introductory workshop at a Zen center. Zen practice is largely a matter of sitting up and paying attention. Through a long tradition extending back to Buddha himself, postures and methods have evolved that help a person wake up and remain alert. Zen meditation is a process of letting go of your usual preoccupation and distractions while opening to what is right here now. The point of Zen is to wake up and live your life fully. I encourage you to experience it for yourself.

## I. ZEN MEDITATION

### Posture

An erect posture is an essential element of Zen meditation. It allows you to be awake and alert with your whole body as well as your mind. You sit up straight without leaning against anything. If you lean or lie down, you are too likely to doze off or daydream. You can sit on a cushion, a meditation bench, or a chair. The cushion or bench is placed on a mat so your knees will be cushioned.

If you sit on a cushion, you sit on the front third of a firm round cushion. Your legs can be crossed in the full lotus position, half lotus position, or with your feet on the mat one in front of the other drawn in close to the cushion. In all of these positions your knees are in contact with the mat so your weight is distributed between your seat on the cushion and your knees on the mat.

If you sit on a bench, kneel with your seat on the bench and your lower legs and feet on the mat. If you are less flexible and need to use a chair, sit with your seat on the front third of the chair and your feet flat on the floor about a foot apart. Do not lean on the back of the chair.

Whether sitting on a cushion, bench, or chair, your pelvis is tilted slightly forward. This opens your abdomen and allows full natural breathing. Also your shoulders are slightly back to open your chest for natural expansion during breathing. Your chin is tucked in slightly and your head is straight over your shoulders.

During Zen meditation your eyes remain open so you do not drift off into dreamland. Your eyes look down at the floor about three feet in front of you or at some Zen centers you sit facing the wall.

Your hands are placed in your lap palms up with your little fingers against your belly. The left hand rests in the right hand. Some sit with the hands in the cosmic mudra with the tips of the thumbs lightly touching each other and the hands forming a horizontal oval. Some have the hands together in the lap with the left hand clasping the right thumb.

Although this posture may seem difficult at first, gradually you will find just the right balance and will be

*Full lotus*

*Half lotus*

*Burmese sitting position*

able to sit straight and relaxed at the same time. During Zen meditation you sit still and do not move, stretch, or fidget. In the stillness and silence your mind and body settle and yet remain awake, alert, and attentive.

## Counting or Attending to the Breath

A good beginning Zen meditation practice is to count your breath. Sit breathing naturally and count each exhalation silently until you reach ten. Then start over with one. The first exhalation count one, the second exhalation count two, and the third exhalation count three. Continue until you notice that your mind has wandered off in thought. At that point, bring your attention back to counting your breath starting over at one. It takes some people many weeks or months before they can get to ten most of the time.

When you find you can get to ten most of the time without wandering off in thought, stop counting your breath and instead just pay attention to your breathing. When you notice you have wandered off in thought, bring your attention back to your breathing. While these simple, but by no means easy, practices are good for beginners, even someone who has been meditating for many years may find returning to counting the breath or paying attention to the breath very helpful from time to time.

## Just Sitting

When you have gotten used to regular periods of meditation, you may want to progress to "just sitting." In "just

*Sitting on a bench*

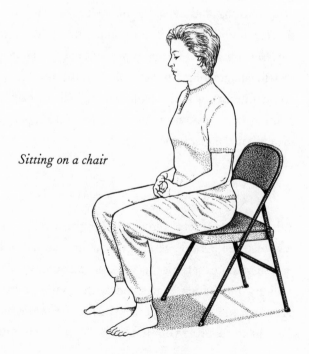

*Sitting on a chair*

sitting" you sit alert and awake, paying attention to the present moment. When you notice your mind has wandered off in thought, you bring your attention back to just sitting right here and now. You don't strain to keep your mind from thinking. You simply choose to come back to the present moment when you notice that you have begun thinking or daydreaming. You choose to return to "just sitting" rather than engaging in your usual thoughts, plans, fantasies, or worries. You don't need to try to clear your mind of thoughts. You just don't add to them or give them your attention. There is plenty of time for thinking and planning later. Right now, during meditation, just sit.

Most people practice Zen meditation for 25 or 30 minutes morning and evening. But you can start out with shorter periods of 10 or 15 minutes and build up gradually. Short periods of regular practice every day are more beneficial than longer periods of sporadic practice. If you are meditating at a Zen center, three bells signal the beginning of a meditation period. The bell rings again at the end of the meditation period.

## II. WALKING ZEN MEDITATION

When a group gets together for Zen practice, you sit for two or three periods of meditation alternating with five or ten minute periods of walking meditation. During walking meditation you stand with your left fist held against your chest at the bottom of the sternum with your right hand covering your left hand. Walk in a straight line following the leader. Your eyes are cast down just as they are during sitting meditation. You follow close behind the person in front of you closing any gaps in the line. The group moves together at the pace set by the leader.

*Walking meditation*

Walking meditation gives you the opportunity to get the circulation in your legs moving again. But walking meditation is not just a break or a stroll. While you are walking your attention is on your walking. When you notice you have started thinking or daydreaming, you bring your attention back to walking right here and now.

Walking meditation helps you learn to be attentive as you go from sitting in meditation to being active in the world. Zen practice does not just occur while sitting in meditation. You become more awake, attentive, and present throughout your daily life. Rather than being preoccupied or engaging in excessive thought or worry you are more aware of life lived each moment.

### III. KOAN PRACTICE

Some branches of Zen also do koan practice. Koans are Zen stories or questions that cannot be understood or answered using the intellect alone. The koans precipitate a shift in perception so you directly experience nonduality, unity, or wholeness. If you are doing koan practice, you work on the koan during meditation and at other times also.

When you think you have seen the point of the koan, you meet with the Zen teacher in an individual meeting to present your understanding. The Zen teacher may encourage you to go deeper or may suggest the next koan for you to work on. People who are practicing counting the breath, attending to the breath, or "just sitting," also may have individual meetings with the Zen teacher to ask questions about their practice and receive individual instruction or encouragement.

# Selected Books and Resources

## Selected Books for Further Reading on Zen

Robert Aitken, *Taking the Path of Zen*. San Francisco: North Point Press, 1982.

Charlotte Joko Beck, edited by Steve Smith, *Everyday Zen: Love and Work*. San Francisco: Harper & Row, 1989.

Bernard Glassman and Rick Fields, *Instructions to the Cook: A Zen Master's Lessons in Living a Life that Matters*. New York: Bell Tower, 1996.

Robert Kennedy, *Zen Gifts to Christians*. New York: Continuum, 2001.

Jean Smith, *The Beginner's Guide to Zen Buddhism*. New York: Bell Tower, 2000.

Shunryu Suzuki, *Zen Mind, Beginner's Mind*. New York: Weatherhill, 1970.

Koun Yamada, *Gateless Gate*. 2d ed. Tucson, AZ: The University of Arizona Press, 1990.

## Selected Books for Further Reading on Healing

Barbara Dossey, Lynn Keegan, and Cathie E. Guzzetta, *Holistic Nursing: A Handbook for Practice*, 3rd ed. Gaithersburg, MD: Aspen, 1999.

Jon Kabat-Zinn, *Full Catastrophe Living*. New York: Delta, 1990.

Rachel Naomi Remen, *Kitchen Table Wisdom: Stories That Heal*. New York: Riverhead, 1997.

Rodney Smith, *Lessons from the Dying*. Boston: Wisdom, 1998.

Jean Watson, *Postmodern Nursing and Beyond*. Edinburgh: Churchill Livingstone, 1999.

## Resources for Ordering Zen Mats, Cushions, and Benches

Dharma Communications
   PO Box 156
   Mount Tremper, NY 12457-0156
   (845) 688-7993
   www.dharma.net/store.html

DharmaCrafts
   405 Waltham Street, Suite 234
   Lexington, Massachusetts 02421
   (800) 794-9862
   www.dharmacrafts.com

Shasta Abbey Buddhist Supplies
   3724 Summit Drive
   Mt. Shasta, CA 96067-9102
   (800) 653-3315
   www.obcon.org

## Selected Zen Centers

The following are Zen Centers I am personally familiar with and recommend:

Lassalle Haus
   Bad Schonbrunn
   Edlibach/Zug CH-6313
   Switzerland
   (041) 757 1414
   www.lassalle-haus.org

Maria Kannon Zen Center
    6532 Hunnicut Rd.
    Dallas, TX 75227
    (214) 388-1122
    www.mkzc.org

Morning Star Zendo
    50 Glenwood Ave.
    Jersey City, NJ 07306
    (201) 985-1515
    www.kennedyzen.com

New River Zen Community
    2121 Charlton Ln.
    Radford, VA 24141
    (540) 639-4109
    www.healingzen.com

Still Mind Zendo
    120 Washington Pl.
    New York, NY 10014
    (212) 414-3128

Upaya Zen Center
    1404 Cerro Gordo Rd.
    Santa Fe, New Mexico 87501
    (505) 986-8518
    www.upaya.org

The Village Zendo
    200 Varick St., Suite 903
    New York, NY 10014
    (212) 340-4656
    www.villagezendo.org

Zen Center of Los Angeles
    923 S. Normandie Ave.
    Los Angeles, CA 90006-1301
    (213) 387-2377
    www.zencenter.com

Zen Community of Baltimore Clare Sangha
    Loveton Center
    53 Loveton Circle #102
    Cockeysville, MD 21030
    (410) 628-6141
    www.zcbclaresangha.org

## Selected Web Sites

The following Web sites include more extensive lists of Zen
centers:

www.peacemakercommunity.org
www.shambhalasun.com
www.tricycle.com

For more information, contact the author at:

Ellen Birx
2121 Charlton Lane
Radford, VA 24141
(540) 639-4109
ebirx@healingzen.com
www.healingzen.com

# Notes

*Page*

*3* My ideas about healing were influenced by nurse theorists Janet Quinn and Jean Watson. See Janet F. Quinn, "Healing: A Model for an Integrative Health Care System." *Advanced Practice Nursing Quarterly*, 3 (1997): pp. 1–7, and also Jean Watson, *Postmodern Nursing and Beyond*. New York: Churchill Livingstone, 1999.

*4* Koun Yamada, *Gateless Gate*. Los Angeles: Center Publications, 1979. Case 35.

*6* "We become compassionate . . ." Huston Smith, *Requiem for a Faith*. Produced by Irving Hartley & Edna Hartley. Cos Cob, CT: Hartley Film Foundation, 1978. Videocassette.

*10* Koun Yamada, op cit., Case 17.

*13* "Lightning flashing . . ." Ibid, p. 112.

*16* Ibid, Case 28.

*22* "I stretch out both legs . . ." Francis H. Cook, tr., *The Record of Transmitting the Light: Zen Master Keizan's Denkoroku*. Los Angeles: Center Publications, 1991: p. 112.

*23* Zen Master Mumon's instructions are from Koun Yamada, op cit., Case 1.

*24* "Sitting long and . . ." Katsuki Sekida, *Two Zen Classics: Mumonkan and Hekiganroku*. New York: Weatherhill, 1977: p. 191.

*28* "Don't draw another's bow . . ." Koun Yamada, op cit., p. 230.

*31* ". . . nothing but trusting the Self." Francis H. Cook, tr., p. 113.

*34* "Mountains and Water Sutra" Gary Snyder (Speaker), *The Teachings of Zen Master Dogen: Selections from Moon in a Dewdrop*. Berkeley, CA: Audio Literature, 1992. Audiocassette.

*35* "Have you eaten your . . ." Koun Yamada, op cit., p. 45.

*36* Marilou Awiatka, *Selu: Seeking the Corn-Mother's Wisdom*. Golden, CO: Fulcrum, 1993.

*40* "The vermillion boat . . ." Francis H. Cook, tr., op cit., p. 196.

*40* "The red of the rustic village . . ." Ibid, p.75.

*42* "I came to realize . . ." Cited in Philip Kapleau, ed., *The Three Pillars of Zen*. Boston: Beacon, 1965: p. 205.

*43* "I, and the great earth . . ." Frances H. Cook, tr., op. cit., p. 27.

*47* "Since I am without . . ." Ibid, p. 93.

*47* "How many times . . ." Ibid, p. 97.

*47* "You must love . . ." Luke 10.27 *The Jerusalem Bible*.

*48* "What is the self . . ." Frances H. Cook, tr., op. cit., p. 212.

*51* "Why is it . . ." Koun Yamada, op. cit., p. 105.

*56* "What is Buddha . . ." Zenkei Shibayama, *Zen Comments on the Mumonkan*. New York: Harper & Row, 1974: p. 134.

*61* "What Is the Way?" Koun Yamada, op. cit., p. 100.

*62* "If you do not see . . ." Zen Peacemaker Order, *Service Book*. Peacemaker Community, P.O. 5391, Santa Barbara, CA 93150, p. 8.

*62* "The spring flowers . . ." Koun Yamada, op. cit., p. 104.

*63* "If you meet a man . . ." Ibid, p. 186.

*65* "How can you expect . . ." Alexander Solzhenitsyn, *One Day in the Life of Ivan Denisovich*. New York: E. P. Dutton, 1963: p. 34.

*66* Story about Hakuin from Zenkei Shibayama, *Zen Comments on the Mumonkan*. New York: Harper & Row, 1974: p. 22.

*68* "What kind of thing . . ." Francis H. Cook, tr., op. cit., p. 39.

*68* "You will know yourself . . ." Koun Yamada, op. cit., p. 14.

*68* "By acquiring the marrow . . ." Frances H. Cook, tr., op. cit., p. 50.

*69* "Dog! Buddha nature . . ." Koun Yamada, op. cit., p. 14.

*75* Story about Master Zuigan from Koun Yamada, ibid., p. 67.

*77* "One has gained . . ." Ibid, p. 137.

*78* "Rolling up the blinds . . ." Katsuki Sekida, op. cit., p. 90.

*78* "I have opened up . . ." From the song "Hallelujah Side." Rev. Johnson Oatman-J. Howard Entwisle (P. D.).

*80* "Afoot and light-hearted . . ." Walt Whitman, *Leaves of Grass*. New York: Random House, 1950/1856: p. 118.

*84* "How will you step . . ." Koun Yamada, op. cit., p. 232.

*84* "Even though one . . ." Ibid, p. 232.

*84* "Foxes have holes . . ." Matthew 8.20 *The Jerusalem Bible*.

*90* "Not knowing is most . . ." Katsuki Sekida, op. cit., p. 90.

*90* "Moonlight reflected in the . . ." Francis H. Cook, tr., op. cit., p. 132.

*91* Hakuyu Taizan Maezumi and Bernard Tetsugen Glassman, *The Hazy Moon of Enlightenment: On Practice III*. Los Angeles: Center Publications, 1978.

*91* "Who pent up the sea . . ." Job 38.8, *The Jerusalem Bible*.

*92* "Who begets the dewdrops?" Ibid., Job 38.28.

*92* "Do you know how . . ." Ibid., Job 39.1.

*92* "I have been holding . . ." Ibid., Job 42.3.

*94* "When emptiness is struck . . ." Francis H. Cook, tr., op. cit., p. 78.

*95* "Even if you are . . ." Ibid, p. 210.

*95* "Seeking it oneself . . ." Ibid, p. 186.

*96* "The spirit of sunyata . . ." Ibid, p. 117.

*97* "If you want to . . ." Ibid, p. 123.

*99* "What is the meaning . . ." Koun Yamada, op. cit., p. 190.

*100* "My late master did . . ." Ibid, p. 192.

*100* "I have come to . . ." Francis H. Cook, tr., op. cit., p. 58.

*101* "I constantly think of . . ." Koun Yamada, op. cit., p. 125.

*105* "How do you see . . ." Francis H. Cook, tr., op. cit., p. 216.

*106* "Form is no other . . ." Zen Peacemaker Order, *Service Book*. Peacemaker Community, P.O. Box 5391, Santa Barbara, CA 93150, 1997: p. 4.

*106* "If you wish to . . ." Francis H. Cook, tr., op. cit., p. 61.

*107* "If in regard to this . . ." Koun Yamada, op. cit., p. 23.

*109* "Did you make your . . ." Francis H. Cook, tr., op. cit., p. 43.

*111* "House demolished, the person . . ." Ibid, p. 46.

*111* "This staff has transformed . . ." Katsuki Sekida, op. cit., p. 312.

*112* "There is no distinction . . ." Francis H. Cook, tr., op. cit., p. 137.

*113* "I and my Father . . ." John 10.30, *King James Version*.

*113* Don Ani Shalom Singer, "The Meaning of 'One' is One." *Sangha Letter: Zen Center of Los Angeles/Buddha Essence Temple*, 23, 5 (1998): p. 4.

*117* "What did the non-Buddhist . . ." Koun Yamada, op. cit., p. 168.

*117* "With realization, all things . . ." Ibid, p. 89.

*119* "Do I contradict myself . . ." Walt Whitman, *Leaves of Grass*, p. 74.

*119* "Under the covers . . ." Peter Matthiessen, *Nine-Headed Dragon River: Zen Journals 1969-1985*. Boston: Shambhala, 1986: p. 23.

*123* "Extremely fine subtle consciousness . . ." Francis H. Cook, tr., op. cit., p. 179.

*124* *Contemporary Perspectives in Philosophy of Religion: An Interview with Willis Harman*. Produced and directed by Arthur Bloch. Oakland, CA: Thinking Allowed Productions, 1988. Videocassette.

*124* "Avoid seeking Him in . . ." Francis H. Cook, tr., op. cit., p. 60.

*125* "Studying Zen is the . . ." Ibid, p. 227.

*126* "Oh, Great Spirit, whose . . ." "Four Winds Native American Medallion." Hazelden Foundation, P.O. Box 176, Center City, MN 55012.

*128* Buddha's six types of suffering are from Huston Smith, *The World's Religions: Our Great Wisdom Traditions*. New York: HarperCollins, 1991.

*129* "Let me respectfully remind . . ." Zen Peacemaker Order, op. cit.

*129* "If when I die . . ." Shunryu Suzuki, *Zen Mind, Beginner's Mind*. New York: Weatherhill, 1997: p. 10.

*130* "I have already put . . ." Francis H. Cook, tr., op. cit., p. 138.

*134* "One can awaken . . ." Koun Yamada, op. cit., p. 214.

*135* "God, grant me the . . ." Reinhold Niebuhr, "The Serenity Prayer." Hazelden Foundation, P.O. Box 176, Center City, MN 55012.

*136* "Keichu made a hundred . . ." Koun Yamada, op. cit., p. 49.

*138* "Thy will be done." Matthew 26.42, *King James Version*.

*145* "Walking on the edge . . ." Koun Yamada, op. cit., p. 169.

*146* "A time for tears . . ." Ecclesiastes 3.4-5, *The Jerusalem Bible*.

*148* "In a sutra it . . ." Koun Yamada, op. cit., p. 242.

*149* "A single hair pierces . . ." Francis H. Cook, tr., op. cit., p. 237.

*149* "Space, from the beginning . . ." Ibid, p. 243.

*153* "Eternity is nothing other . . ." Koun Yamada, op. cit., p. 237.

*154* "Daitsu Chisho Buddha sat . . ." Ibid, p. 54.

*155* "How do you feel . . ." Katsuki Sekida, op. cit., p. 152.

*159* "Not thinking of good . . ." Francis H. Cook, tr., op. cit., pp. 154–155.

*163* "During the last forty-eight . . ." Anna H. Shaw, *The Story of a Pioneer*. New York: Harper Brothers, 1929: p. 233.

*165* "All the great world . . ." Katsuki Sekida, op. cit., p. 159.

*172* "We experienced the subtle . . ." Ibid., p. 351.

*173* "Seeking it oneself with . . ." Francis H. Cook, tr., *The Record of Transmitting the Light: Zen Master Keizan's Denkoroku*. Los Angeles: Center Publications, 1991: p. 186.

*173* Information on Kannon from Ruben L. F. Habito, *Total Liberation: Zen Spirituality and the Social Dimension*. New York: Orbis, 1989: p. 102.

*174* "Barechested, barefooted, he comes . . ." Philip Kapleau, ed. *The Three Pillars of Zen*. Boston: Beacon, 1965: p. 323.

*176* Information on ox-herding pictures from ibid.

*176* Richard J. Lowry, ed., *The Journals of A. H. Maslow:* Volume II. Monterey, CA: Brooks/Cole, 1979.

*179* "The body is the . . ." Francis H. Cook, tr., op. cit., p. 152.

*179* "Enlightenment is essentially not . . ." Ibid, p. 153.

*186* "How can something that . . ." Ibid., p. 223.

*186* "What thing will you . . ." Ibid, p. 127.

*190* "Seeing, hearing, forms, and . . ." Ibid, p. 147.

*190* "Joshu Sees Through an . . ." Koun Yamada, op. cit., p. 163.

*195* "Who can hear the . . ." Francis H. Cook, tr., op. cit., p. 174.

*195* "Wonderful! Wonderful! The preaching . . ." Ibid, p. 174.

*196* "Are the bells ringing . . ." Ibid, p. 98.

*197* "The Dharma of the . . ." Koun Yamada, op. cit., p. 131.

*202* "I am solitary and . . ." Ibid, p. 58.

*204* "Because it is so . . ." Zenkei Shibayama, *Zen Comments on the Mumonkan*. New York: Harper & Row, 1974: p. 70.

*206* "If one of you . . ." Ibid., p. 76.

*207* "What is Buddha?" Ibid, p. 109.

*208* "How is my hand . . ." Ibid, p. 253.

*208*  "Groping for the pillow . . ." Ibid, p. 253.

*212*  "Buddha spoke with a . . ." Francis H. Cook, tr., op. cit., p. 219.

*218*  "Father and mother are . . ." Ibid, p. 6.

*222*  "I beg you in . . ." Ibid, p. 145.

*223*  "When a carp in . . ." Koun Yamada, op. cit., p. 242.

*223*  "Gateless is the Great . . ." Zenkei Shibayama, op. cit., p. 10.

*223*  Marsha M. Linehan, *Cognitive-Behavioral Treatment of Borderline Disorder.* New York: Guilford, 1993.

*231*  "Even Shakyamuni and Maitreya . . ." Koun Yamada, op. cit., p. 227.

*232*  "He now is surely . . ." Francis H. Cook, tr., op. cit., p. 60.

*232*  Discussion of four types of people from Koun Yamada, op. cit., p. 134.

*233*  "The world is vast . . ." Katsuki Sekida, op. cit., p. 65.

*237*  "Let there be peace . . ." Sy Miller and Jill Jackson, "Let There Be Peace On Earth." Jan-Lee Music, P.O. Box 4, West Charleston, VT 05872.

*237*  "Your disciple's mind is . . ." Koun Yamada, op. cit., p. 208.

*238*  "Liberated, he is mild . . ." Francis H. Cook, tr., op. cit.,  p. 227.

*242*  Buddha's analogy of a fine horse is from Koun Yamada, op. cit., p. 170.

*244*  "The ancients said . . ." Francis H. Cook, tr., op. cit., p. 187.

# Index